JAZZ GUITAR VOICINGS
VOL 1: THE DROP 2 BOOK

BY RANDY VINCENT
(Adapted from Mark Levine's "The Drop 2 Book")

Music Engraving - Chuck Gee
Cover Graphics - Attila Nagy
Cover Artwork - Sueann Bettison Sher
Cover Photos - Kathy Vincent

Table of Contents

Dedication

To my teacher the late Park Hill, my guitar heroes including Jim Hall, Wes Montgomery, and George Benson among many others, and my harmonic inspirations Thelonious Monk, Barry Harris, Bill Evans, Herbie Hancock, Debussy, Stravinsky, etc. etc. etc.

Acknowledgments

SPECIAL THANKS TO:
Chuck Sher, for his encouragement and for making this project possible.
Mark Levine, for creating the idea for this book in the first place.
Chuck Gee, for the fantastic music engraving and great advice.

About the Author

Randy Vincent has had a long and illustrious career in jazz. He has performed, toured and/or recorded with Dizzy Gillespie, Joe Henderson, Bobby Hutcherson, Bebop And Beyond, The Turtle Island String Quartet, and many others.

Randy has taught jazz guitar at Sonoma State University since 1981 and has conducted clinics throughout the US and overseas. Some of his more well-known former students include Julian Lage, Dave MacNab, Chris Pimentel, and Liberty Ellmen. He currently teaches at Sonoma State University and privately.

He has performed at numerous jazz festivals including the Monterey Jazz Festival and Dizzy Gillespie's 75th birthday celebration at the Hollywood Bowl, as well as performing regularly with the Santa Rosa Symphony's Pops Concerts.

A selected discography of Randy's recordings:
>> Randy Vincent - "Nisha's Dream" and "Mirror Image"
>> Bobby Hutcherson - "Ambos Mundos"
>> Bebop And Beyond - "Bebop And Beyond Plays Dizzy Gillespie" (featuring Dizzy)
>>>> and "Bebop And Beyond Plays Thelonious Monk" (featuring Joe Henderson)
>> Stephanie Ozer - "O Comeco" (featuring Leny Andrade)
>> Larry Baskett Trio - "Chalice" and "Poor Boy Blue"
>> Mel Graves - "Emotion In Motion"
>> Turtle Island String Quartet - "Spider Dreams"
>> Peter Welker - "Para Peachy", "We'll Be Together Again" and "Shining Hour"
>> Vern Thompson - "Passions Of The Heart", "Sea Of Dreams" and "Convergence"
>>>> (featuring Bob Sheppard, Akira Tana, Tony Dumas and Billy Childs)
>> Mike Vax Big Band - "Alternate Route"
>> Dave Eshelman's Garden Big Band - "Milagro's Journey"

About This Book

I was practicing my guitar one day (just like every other day) when the phone rang. I answered thinking it might be a gig, but instead it was Chuck Sher saying he just got a call from Mark Levine, author of *The Jazz Piano Book, The Jazz Theory Book,* and *Jazz Piano Masterclass - The Drop 2 Book*. Mark said that a guitarist had called to report that he had learned more about harmony from Mark's Drop 2 book than he had from any guitar book. Well, I have to agree, as I've had the same experience with all of Mark's books. Mark and Chuck discussed the possibility of a guitar version of the Drop 2 book, and then Chuck gave me a call. He had been encouraging me to write something for a while, but I just kept practicing and playing. This time, however, with a specific concept in mind, I decided to take him up on his offer. Chuck gave me the freedom to borrow freely from Mark's work, as well as the freedom to expand on the concept and make it my own contribution.

This book focuses on drop 2 voicings for jazz guitar, and only uses examples of other types of voicings to clarify our understanding of the nature and usefulness of the drop 2 system. Therefore the "Vol.1" in the title, so we can cover many other equally interesting and useful concepts in the future. The chapter layout is roughly patterned after Mark's book, and like Mark's book the concept is explained and defined by examples in the body of the text. Like most things worth doing, this book will require a lot of hard work, but the results will be most rewarding.

About Guitar Notation and Chord Diagrams

This book uses standard guitar music notation supplemented with standard fingerboard diagrams to help make it easier for less experienced readers to determine where to finger the voicings. Guitar music sounds one octave lower than written (compared to piano music), enabling the music to be written entirely in treble clef. Occasionally (such as Example 1-1) the music will be marked 8va, making it sound an octave higher than standard guitar pitch. This is usually done to reduce the number of high ledger lines, making the voicings easier to read. In the fingerboard diagrams the vertical lines represent the strings (low E-A-D-G-B-high E left to right) while the horizontal lines represent the frets, with the lowest fingered fret numbered on the upper right side of each diagram. When a chord is played in the first or open position, the heavier horizontal line across the top of the diagram represents the nut. Fingerings are not given because many of the forms can only be played one way, while the others should be fingered the way that works best for you.

Definition of Drop 2

The term "drop 2" refers to a type of four-note chord voicing played by piano or guitar that is derived from a "four-way close voicing." A four-way close voicing is a four-note chord with the notes spanning less than the range of an octave, making them as close together in pitch as possible. The drop 2 voicings are derived from four-way close voicings by lowering the second highest note by one octave. This opens the voicing and makes it practical to play on four consecutive strings on the guitar.

CHAPTER 1 - GETTING STARTED WITH DROP 2

Play Example 1-1 (CD1 Track #1), the first four bars of Kenny Dorham's "Blue Bossa". This is the sound of drop 2.

Ex. 1-1

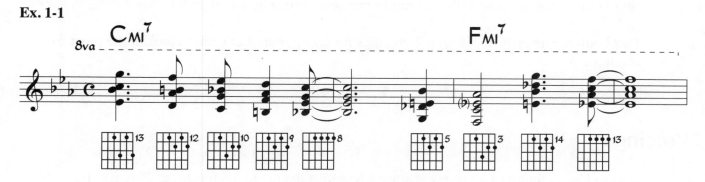

Play Ex. 1-2 (CD1 Track #2), the same four bars of "Blue Bossa", this time with drop 2 tweaked a bit to make it sound more interesting.

Ex. 1-2

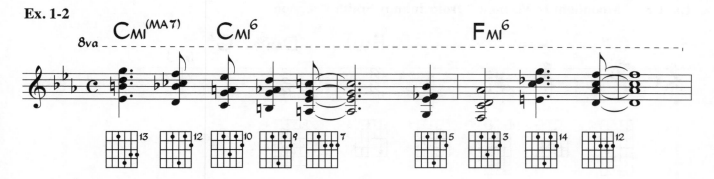

This book covers both the basic version of drop 2, demonstrated in Ex. 1-1 and the more advanced version shown in Ex. 1-2.

Block Chords

The previous fragments are examples of what arrangers and jazz musicians commonly refer to as "block chords". The term refers to having a similarly voiced "block" of harmony under each note of a melody. Notice I said "under each note of a melody". Block chords build the harmony from the top down, rather than from the bass note up, and are usually used in conjunction with another instrument supplying the bass line. This way the melody is the highest, or soprano, voice in the chord. The melody may be the melody of a tune, or part of an improvised solo line, or a background melody accompanying a tune or solo played by someone else.

You need to know at least a little jazz harmony to make sense of this book: chord construction (the notes that make up a given chord), and the II-V-I progression.

Block chords frequently involve four voices, the melody note and three harmony notes, that move in approximate parallel motion, keeping the spacing between the notes roughly similar. However, the voicing types used may vary. For instance a block chord passage may use all 4-way close voicings, or all drop 2 voicings, or all Shearing Style, etc. A passage in drop 2, for instance, may have an occasional 4-way close or an occasional drop 3 without compromising the block chord effect, but in general it's best not to randomly mix a bunch of widely contrasting voicings.

This book is primarily about drop 2 voicings for jazz guitar. Let's take a look at the types of voicings.

Voicings

4-way close is four part harmony spanning less than the range of an octave. Play Ex. 1-3 (CD1 Track #3), close voicings as played on guitar by Johnny Smith on his famous recording of "Moonlight in Vermont" featuring Stan Getz. Notice the difficult left hand stretches required to play close harmonies on guitar.

Ex. 1-3   "Moonlight In Vermont" from Johnny Smith's version

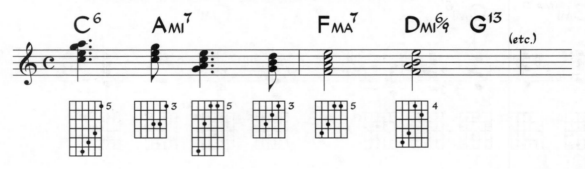

Ex. 1-4 (CD1 Track #4) is the C Bebop Major Scale in 4-way close, worked out using open strings whenever possible to make it playable on guitar.

Ex. 1-4   C Bebop Major Scale in 4-way close

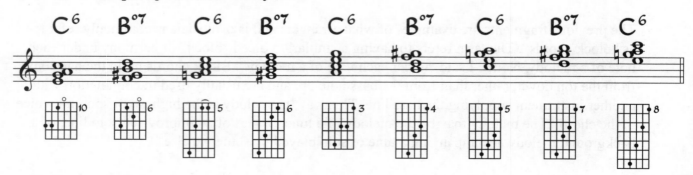

Still pretty tough isn't it? Try changing keys and you're in for some serious challenges.

By the way, the C Bebop Major Scale is a C Major scale with an added note (G# or Ab) making it an 8 note scale. Every other note, the first, third, fifth, and seventh notes spell out a C6 chord. The other notes, the second, fourth, sixth, and eighth notes spell out a diminished 7th chord, which being symmetrical, could be named Bdim7, Ddim7, Fdim7, or Abdim7. The Bdim7 chord can be analyzed as the 3rd, 5th, 7th, and b9th of a G7b9 chord. The harmonies we will be using treat the root, 3rd, 5th and 6th as chord tones and the 2nd, 4th, flat 6th and 7th as passing tones. The chord tones will be harmonized with a C6 chord and the passing tones harmonized with the diminished 7th chord that represents the V7b9 chord.

Shearing Style voicings are piano voicings named after pianist George Shearing, who popularized the style in the 1950s, although the voicings can be traced back to arrangers writing for 5-part sax sections. It was originally 4-way close with the fifth part being baritone sax doubling the melody played by the lead alto sax, but one octave lower. Obviously, considering the difficulty of 4-way close on the guitar, the Shearing voicings will be impossible. However, they can be simulated by leaving out one of the inner voices, as in Ex. 1-5 (CD1 Track #5). These are simulated Shearing Style voicings for guitar playing the C Bebop Major Scale.

Ex. 1-5   C Bebop Major Scale in simulated Shearing Style

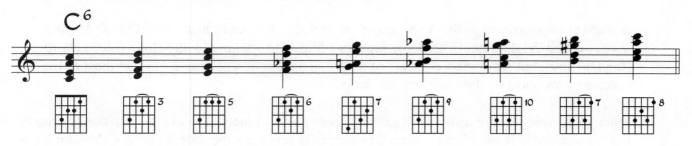

Drop 2 voicings not only sound good on piano but are a great and practical solution to the close voicing problems on guitar. Drop 2 means lowering the 2nd voice from the top of a close voicing by one octave. This opens up the voicing and makes it easy to play on guitar.

Try Ex. 1-6 of the C Bebop Major Scale in drop 2 (CD1 Track #6).

Ex. 1-6   C Bebop Major Scale in Drop-2

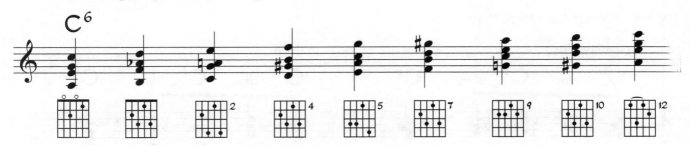

O.K., so like most things it's going to require a lot of practice, but you can see that all the voicings are quite playable. Notice that all but the first and last voicings in the example use the same fingers on the same strings, so don't lift the fingers off the strings, just slide and reconfigure their spacing as you go. This happens a lot with drop 2 voicings on the middle four strings of the guitar, but not so much on the top four or bottom four. Now try Ex. 1-7 (CD1 Track #7) from Wes Montgomery's recording of Dave Brubeck's "In Your Own Sweet Way" from *The Incredible Jazz Guitar of Wes Montgomery*.

Ex. 1-7   "In Your Own Sweet Way" from Wes Montgomery's version

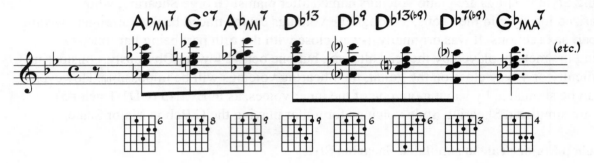

It starts at measure five of the A section of the melody. It's really just a II-V-I in Gb Major. Wes tweaked the dominant chord voicings, in addition to slipping in one close voiced chord (the Db13b9), but it's a good example of an actual application of drop 2. In fact most of the voicings Wes plays on the recording are drop 2.

Since close voicings are difficult on guitar it's not always practical to use them to create drop 2, but we can verify if any chord is drop 2 by mentally reversing the drop 2 process. You imagine that the lowest note of your chord is raised one octave. If it would now be the second highest note, it's drop 2. However, let's say it turns out to be the third highest note, that means it's actually drop 3. Many generic jazz guitar chords are actually drop 3. Typically drop 2 chords cover four adjacent strings while drop 3 are usually distributed across five strings with one string skipped.

Now play Ex. 1-8 (CD1 Track #8), the first bar of Duke Ellington's "What Am I Here For?", first in 4-way close, then in drop 2.

Ex. 1-8   "What Am I Here For?"

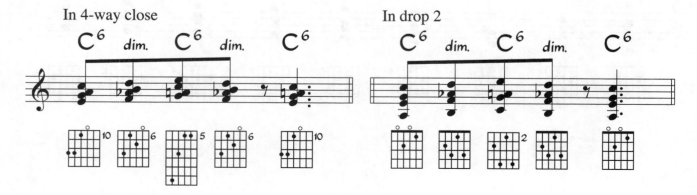

If you were to continue the tune in 4-way close, or even change the key of the first bar, it would become evident that 4-way close is not very practical on guitar. Continue the tune in drop 2 and you'll see there is no problem. However, we'll first have to learn how to handle other chord types besides major. We'll get to that soon.

Ex. 1-9 (CD1 Track #9) shows the first four bars of Irving Berlin's classic "Always", shown in drop 2. Every note is a chord tone of Ab6, except for the Bb (the 9th), which is voiced as a diminished chord.

Ex. 1-9   "Always" in Drop-2

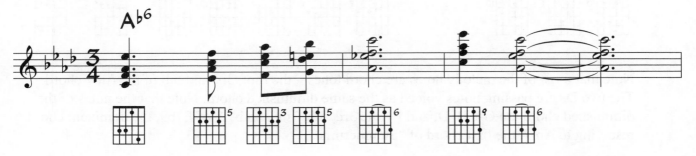

The Bebop Natural Minor Scale

Play Ex. 1-10 (CD1 Track #10), the A Bebop Natural Minor Scale in drop 2.

Ex. 1-10   A Bebop Natural Minor Scale in Drop-2

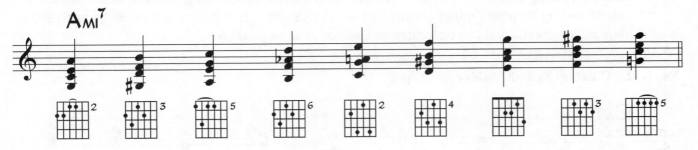

Notice that it contains the same notes as the C Bebop Major Scale and is harmonized with the same voicings. This happens because the C6 chord and the Am7 chord are identical, only with a different note functioning as the root. The two scales - C bebop major, and A bebop natural minor - have exactly the same intervallic relationship as do major and relative minor keys: the natural minor is a minor 3rd below the major. Note that the chromatic passing note (G#) is the same in both scales, except that it occurs between the seventh and eighth notes in the bebop natural minor scale, and between the fifth and sixth notes of the bebop major scale.

As an example of the Bebop Natural Minor Scale, Ex. 1-11 (CD1 Track #11) shows the first few bars of George Gershwin's classic "Summertime" in drop 2.

Ex. 1-11   "Summertime" using Bebop Natural Minor in Drop-2

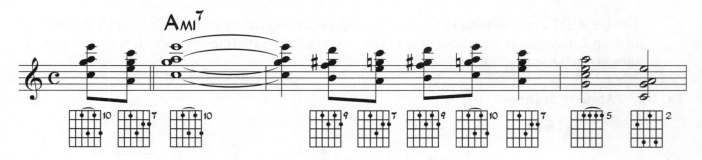

Note that most of the melody notes are chord tones – the root, 3rd and 5th of the Am7 chord. The two Ds are passing notes voiced as the same diminished chord. Note that the notes of the diminished chord are G#, B, D, and F - the 3rd, 5th, 7th, and b9th of E7b9, the dominant chord resolving to Am7, the first chord of "Summertime".

The Bebop Melodic Minor Scale

In addition to the Bebop Natural Minor Scale some minor chords maybe be harmonized with the Bebop Melodic Minor Scale, a melodic minor scale with a chromatic passing note between the fifth and sixth scale steps. Let's look at C Bebop Melodic Minor since it's identical to the C bebop major scale except for the minor third, so to harmonize it we simply flat the E's making each C6 voicing a Cm6. Play Ex. 1-12 (CD1 Track #12), the C bebop melodic minor scale voiced in drop 2 . Many minor chords that are not part of a II-V progression may be analyzed as *tonic minor* chords and can be treated as Cm6 or even as CmMaj7.

Ex. 1-12   C Bebop Melodic Minor in Drop-2

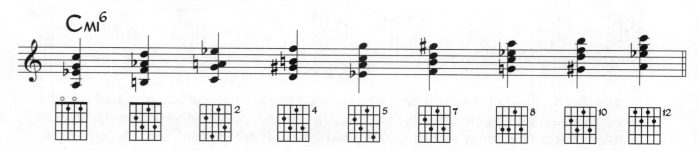

Let's take a look back at "Summertime". Notice that the 7th of the Am7 chord does not appear in this portion of the melody. Since the song is in the key of A minor we could certainly treat the A minor as a tonic minor chord. Play this variation, Ex. 1-13 (CD1 Track #13), of "Summertime" in A bebop melodic minor scale voiced in drop 2.

Ex. 1-13   "Summertime" using Bebop Melodic Minor in Drop-2

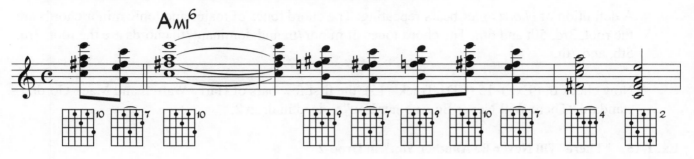

Later on we'll return to "Summertime" for another variation demonstrating a more modern, "modal" concept on the tonic minor 6th chord.

The Bebop Dominant Scale

Play Ex. 1-14 (CD1 Track #14), the C Bebop Dominant Scale in drop 2. If you're familiar with jazz harmony, this is the same as the scale known as the C Mixolydian mode, except that it has a chromatic passing note - B natural - between the seventh and final note of the scale.

Ex. 1-14   C Bebop Dominant Scale in Drop-2

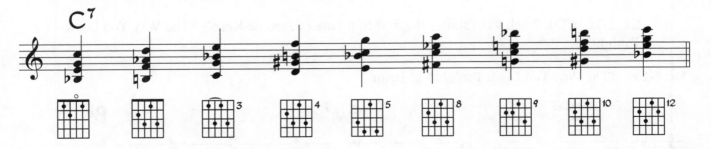

Note that, unlike the other bebop scales, one of the four diminished chords is different from the other three. The first, second, and fourth diminished chords are the same chord - F, Ab, B, D - in different inversions. The notes of the third diminished chord are completely different - C, Eb, F#, and A. It is nothing to worry about, but something you should notice.

Voicing Tunes in Drop 2

The basic rules for voicing melodies in drop 2 are simple:

1) Voice chord tones as major, minor7, tonic minor, or dominant chords
2) Voice passing notes as diminished chords.

A definition of *chord tones* bears repeating: The chord tones of major and tonic minor chords are the root, 3rd, 5th and 6th. The chord tones of minor7th and dominant7th chords are the root, 3rd, 5th, and 7th.

Now check out Ex. 1-15 (CD1 Track #15), the first few bars of Harry Warren and Mack Gordon's standard "There Will Never Be Another You" voiced in drop 2.

Ex. 1-15 "There Will Never Be Another You" in Drop-2

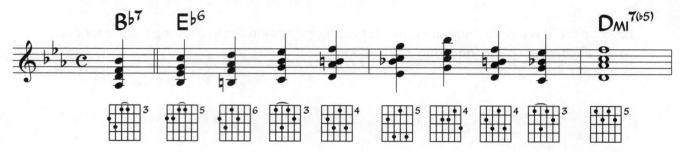

Looking at the Eb6 chord, the melody notes C, Eb, G, and Bb are all chord tones, the 6th, root, 3rd, and 5th respectively. They are all harmonized with inversions of Eb6 chords. The melody notes D and F are passing tones harmonized with diminished chords. The final F is a chord tone of the D *half-diminished*, a fancy name for Dm7b5.

Here are some more fragments of tunes, voiced in drop 2.

Ex. 1-16 (CD1 Track #16) shows the first four bars of Jerome Kern's "The Way You Look Tonight".

Ex. 1-16 "The Way You Look Tonight" in Drop-2

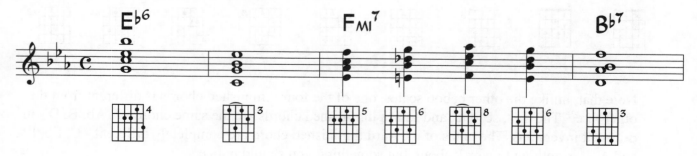

Ex. 1-17 (CD1 Track #17) shows the pickups to Johnny Mandel's "The Shadow Of Your Smile". There's a new chord in the passage that we'll explain in Chapter 2.

Ex. 1-17   "The Shadow Of Your Smile" in Drop-2

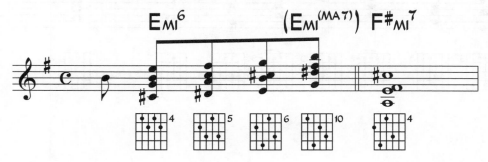

The first two bars of the bridge of Sigmund Romberg's "Lover Come Back To Me" are shown in Ex. 1-18 (CD1 Track #18).

Ex. 1-18   "Lover Come Back To Me" in Drop-2

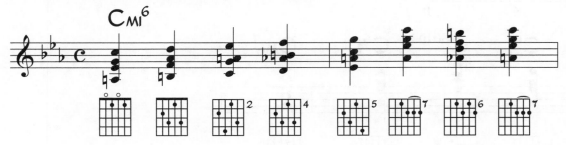

Most of the examples so far have been fragments of tunes that feature a lot of scale-wise melodic motion since these lend themselves to the system of voicings we've been using.

It would be very rare to be able to voice an entire tune using the rules we've been following so far. There may be various reasons why this is so, but one of the main reasons is the frequent necessity to treat notes that our rules tell us are non-chord tones as chord tones. These are chord extensions that do not act as passing notes but must be treated as harmonic tones. Therefore, we need a collection of drop 2 voicings that harmonize these chord extensions. For now, try Ex. 1-19 (bars 5, 6 & 7 of "There Will Never Be Another You") on the following page to hear how our non-chord tone harmonized by diminished 7th rule yields an unusable result (version A), while treating the C in bar 7 as the 9th of a Bbm9 chord (version B) sounds great (CD1 Track #19).

Ex. 1-19

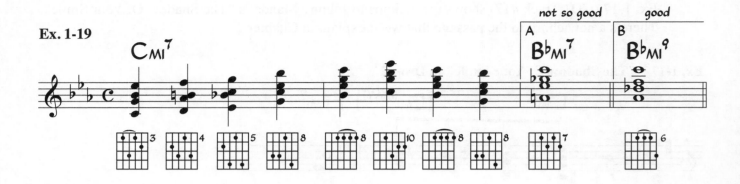

Here's a collection of voicings for common extensions on major chords, minor 7 chords, tonic minor chords and dominant 7 chords. On major chords the common extensions are Maj7, 9 and #11. The voicings in Ex. 1-20 (CD1 Track #20) are modified from our standard drop 2 Maj6 voicings so as to retain the major 3rd while harmonizing the Maj7, 9 and #11.

Ex. 1-20

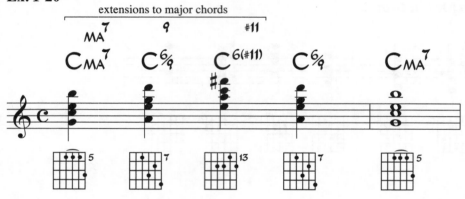

On minor 7 chords the common extensions are 9, 11, and 13. The voicings in Ex. 1-21 (CD1 Track #21) are modified drop 2 minor 7 voicings chosen to keep the minor 3rd and minor 7th while harmonizing the 9, 11 and 13.

Ex. 1-21

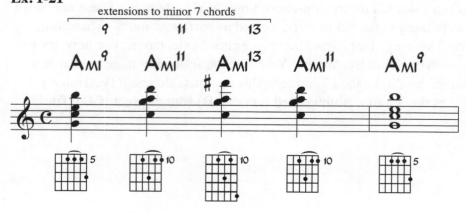

On tonic minor chords the common extensions are Maj7, 9 and 11. The voicings in Ex. 1-22 (CD1 Track #22) are modified drop 2 min6 voicings keeping the minor 3rd while harmonizing the Maj7, 9 and 11.

Ex. 1-22

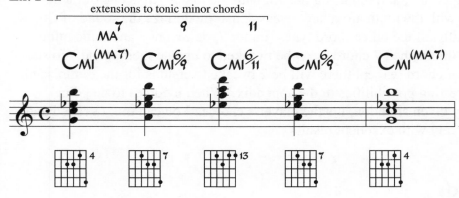

The common extensions on dominant 7 chords are 9, #11 and 13. The voicings in Ex. 1-23 (CD1 Track #23) harmonize these extensions while retaining the major 3rd and minor 7th that define the dominant 7 sound.

Ex. 1-23

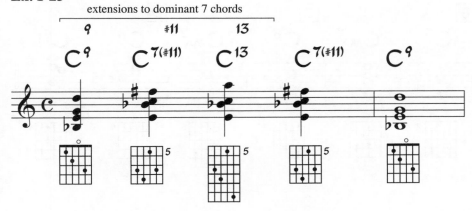

By the way, you may be wondering about Altered Dominant chords and extensions. For now, if we encounter Alt chords we will substitute our standard dominant 7 and dominant 7 extension voicings a tritone away. For example, if a melody note is the #5 of a G Alt, substitute a Db9 extension voicing (the 9 of Db is Eb, the #5 of G). If it's the #9 of a G Alt, substitute a Db13 extension voicing (the 13 of Db is Bb, the #9 of G).

Incidentally, all these extension and substitute voicings are still, strictly speaking, drop 2 voicings. Check it out. As I mentioned earlier you can mentally raise the lowest note of each chord by one octave to verify that it would then become the second highest note of a 4-way close voicing.

CHAPTER 2 - TWEAKING DROP 2

The major chords we have used so far have all been major 6th chords, rather than the usual (in jazz harmony) major 7th chords. There are various ways to make major chords sound more modern when playing drop 2, and replacing the 6th with the major 7th is one of them. Replacing the root or third with the ninth are other "tweaks" that modernize the sound of C6 by making it a C6/9. Actually all the other chord types (minor 7, dominant 7 and tonic minor 6, along with their passing diminished 7 chords) can be tweaked to update their sound. To start we'll only list one tweak per chord (except there will be 2 tweaked versions for the diminished 7), but we'll list other interesting possibilities in the appendix. When it comes to deciding what to actually play in any given situation, it's the player's choice. You can mix tweaked and standard drop 2 voicings freely with excellent results.

Tweaking Major Chords

Ex. 2-1 (CD1 Track #24) shows all four C6 chords in drop 2, as you played them in chapter 1, along with a tweaked version for each. These demonstrate how changing one note can create a richer chord. The examples are each two bars: The bar on the left shows the traditional drop 2 version of the chord; the bar on the right the tweaked version, with one note raised or lowered.

Ex. 2-1   Tweaking major chords

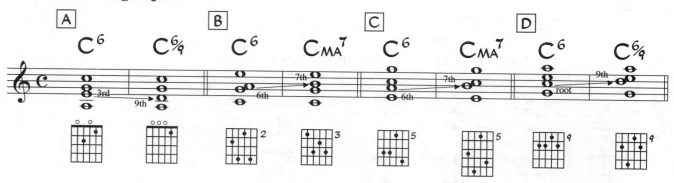

Look at the first bar of 2-1a: the C6 chord with C (the root) in the melody. In the next bar, E, the 3rd of C6, has been dropped a whole step to D, the 9th. This creates a chord in which the notes are a perfect fourth away from each adjacent note. These *fourth chords* were first made popular by pianist McCoy Tyner back in the early 1960s, but are easy to play and sound great on the guitar. The D in the voicing is the 9th of the chord, hence the chord symbol C6/9.

Look at Ex. 2-1b, the C6 chord in the first bar has E (the 3rd) in the melody. In the following bar, the note A (the 6th) has been raised a whole step to B, the major 7th, creating a Cmajor7th chord (sometimes notated as CΔ).

In Ex. 2-1c, the C6 chord in the first bar has G, the 5th, in the melody. In the 2nd bar, A, the 6th, has been raised a whole step to B, the major 7th, creating another CMaj7 chord.

In Ex. 2-1d, the C6 chord in the first bar has A, the 6th, in the melody. In the second bar, C, the root, has been raised a whole step to D, the 9th, which yields another C6/9, an inversion of a fourth chord.

Tweaking Diminished Chords

The diminished chords that you have been playing sound a bit old-fashioned, sort of like the chords announcing the entrance of a silent movie villain.

Fortunately, it is easy to make diminished chords sound more modern. Just follow this rule: In drop 2, *you can raise either the second or third note from the top in a diminished chord by a whole step.*

Ex. 2-2 (CD1 Track #25) shows the tweaked diminished chords. Ex. 2-2A shows the diminished chords with the third note from the top raised by a whole step. Ex. 2-2B shows the diminished chords with the second note from the top raised by a whole step.

Ex. 2-2 Tweaking diminished chords

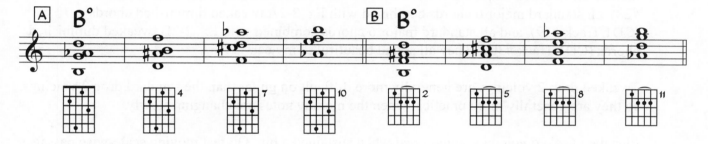

The Bebop Major Scale Tweaked

Now play Ex. 2-3 (CD1 Track #26), the C Bebop Major Scale in tweaked drop 2.

Ex. 2-3 C Bebop Major Scale in Tweaked Drop-2

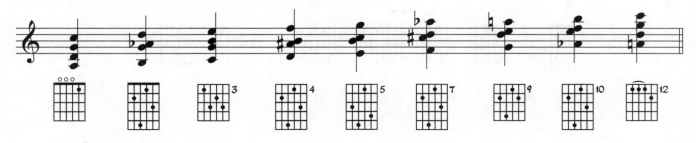

The previous example uses the four tweaked major chords from Ex. 2-1 combined with the tweaked diminished chords from Ex. 2-2A. Compare with Ex. 2-4 (CD1 Track #27), which combines the same tweaked major chords with the tweaked diminished chords from Ex. 2-2B.

Ex. 2-4   C Bebop Major Scale in Tweaked Drop-2

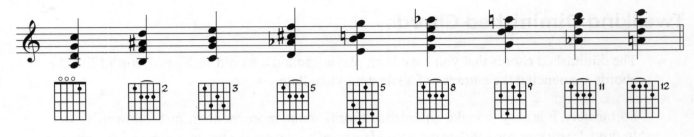

Actually you could mix different tweaked diminished chords for different scale degrees according to your own individual taste. Experiment. Also compare tweaked drop 2 scales with standard drop 2 scales.

You can experiment with mixing standard and tweaked as well. Some combinations to try would include all tweaked major chords combined with all standard diminished chords (CD1 Track #28), all standard major 6 chords combined with Ex. 2-2A tweaked diminished chords (CD1 Track #29), and all standard major 6 chords combined with Ex. 2-2B tweaked diminished chords (CD1 Track #30). They all sound beautiful to my ear.

Tweaked drop 2 voicings are generally more difficult on guitar than the standard drop 2 voicings, so they are generally more practical when the melody notes are changing slowly.

Plus the tweaked voicings sound great when sustained a bit. On fast moving scale-wise passages the standard voicings will usually sound fine. Of course when the melody lands on a sustained note you can switch to a tweaked voicing if you like.

Ex. 2-5 (CD1 Track #31) is the same melody fragment from "Always" that we played in standard drop 2 in Ex. 1-9, but with all the chords tweaked.

Ex. 2-5   "Always" in Tweaked Drop-2

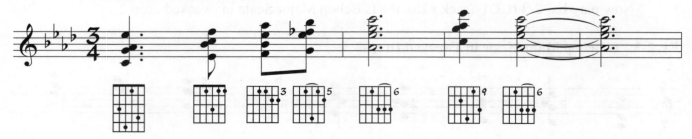

Tweaking Dominant Chords

Ex. 2-6 (CD1 Track #32) shows all four C7 chords in drop 2 as we played them in chapter 1, along with their tweaked versions. In Ex. 2-6A and 2-6B, the note G, the 5th, has been raised a whole step, becoming A, the 13th in the following bars. In Ex. 2-6C and in 2-6D, the note C, the root, has been raised a whole step, becoming D, the 9th in the following bars.

Ex. 2-6   Tweaking dominant chords

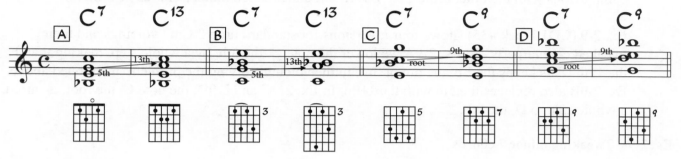

Now play Ex. 2-7 (CD1 Track #33), the C Bebop Dominant Scale in tweaked drop 2. The tweaked C7 chords are all from Ex. 2-6 while the tweaked diminished chords are from Ex. 2-2A.

Ex. 2-7   C Bebop Dominant Scale in Tweaked Drop-2

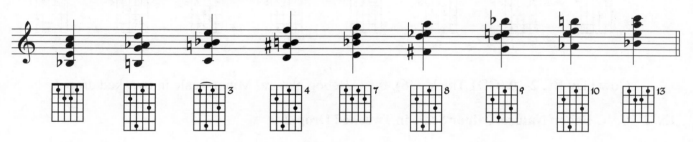

Ex. 2-8 (CD1 Track #34) is the same C Bebop Dominant Scale in tweaked drop 2 using the same tweaked C7 chords, but this time the tweaked diminished chords are from Ex. 2-2B.

Ex. 2-8   C Bebop Dominant Scale in Tweaked Drop-2

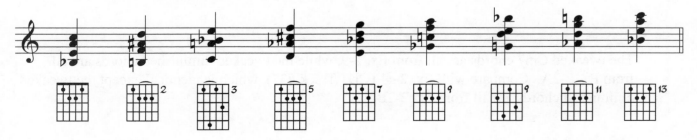

Compare these with each other and with the standard drop 2 version from chapter 1, Try mixing them up again. Experiment and discover your own favorite combinations.

Tweaking Minor 7 Chords

You might be wondering if we can use the tweaked version of the C Bebop Major Scale as a tweaked A Bebop Natural Minor Scale since the standard drop 2 voicings for A Bebop Natural Minor were identical to the standard drop 2 voicings for C Bebop Major. Well, it almost works but the tweaked voicing C6/9 from Ex. 2-1D doesn't really make a convincing A minor voicing because it has no minor 3rd and it sounds too much like A7sus4. For reasons of range and comparisons with the other scales, let's work out our tweaked minor7 chords in C minor.

Ex. 2-9 (CD1 Track #35) shows four inversions for standard drop 2 Cm7 voicings and their tweaked counterparts. In Ex. 2-9A we lower the note G, the 5th, by a whole step, making it an F, the 11th. This keeps the Eb, the minor 3rd, in the voicing, solving the problem mentioned above. Ex. 2-9B also replaces the 5th with the 11th. In Ex. 2-9C and 2-9D, the note C, the root, is raised a whole step to D, the 9th.

Ex. 2-9   Tweaking minor 7 chords

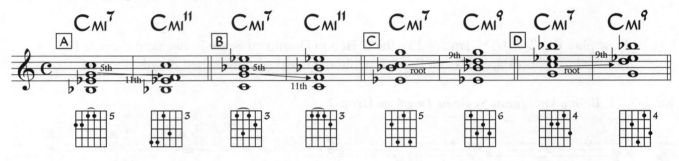

Now play Ex. 2-10 (CD1 Track #36), the C Bebop Natural Minor Scale in tweaked drop 2.

Ex. 2-10   C Bebop Natural Minor Scale in Tweaked Drop-2

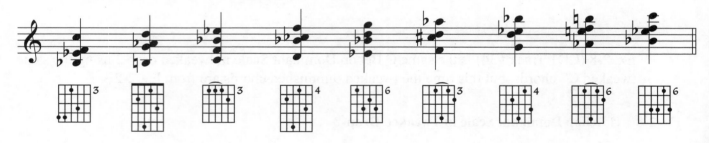

The tweaked Cm7 chords are all from Ex. 2-9, while the tweaked diminished chords are all from Ex. 2-2A. Compare with Ex. 2-11 (CD1 Track #37), which is identical except the tweaked diminished chords are all from Ex. 2-2B.

Ex. 2-11   C Bebop Natural Minor Scale in Tweaked Drop-2

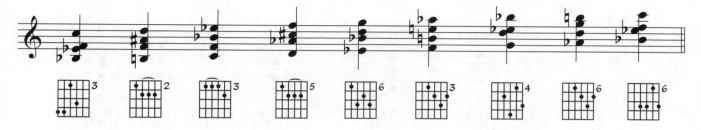

Again, compare these with the standard drop 2 from chapter 1 transposed to C minor, and experiment with various combinations.

Tweaking Tonic Minor Chords

There are two types of minor chords, defined by their function.

1) a minor 7th chord that is part of a II-V progression is called a *II chord.* Dm7 is a II chord when followed by G7, the V chord in the same key. The two chords form the Dm7 G7 progression, the II-V progression in the key of C.

2) a minor7th chord that is not part of a II-V progression is usually a *tonic minor* chord, also known as a *minor I* chord. Dm7 followed by any chord other than G7 is often reharmonized as Dm6 or DmMaj7. II chords are minor 7th chords; V chords are dominant 7th chords. Tonic minor chords are I chords.

Now play the first example in this book again, Ex. 1-1, shown here as Ex. 2-12 (CD1 Track #38). This is a correct way to play "Blue Bossa" in drop 2, but it's not the only way. Jazz musicians love to reharmonize. The first chord is shown as Cm7. That frequently indicates a II chord, which is usually followed by a V chord in the same key. In this case, Cm7 would be followed by F7 - but it isn't. This means it might sound better as a Cm6 chord. The same is true for the Fm7 chord in the third bar. It is not followed by Bb7, so it might sound better to play it as Fm6.

Ex. 2-12   "Blue Bossa" using Bebop Natural Minor Scales in Drop-2

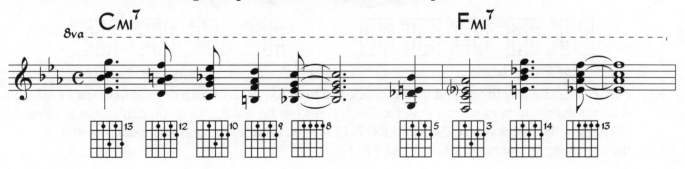

Ex. 2-13 (CD1 Track #39) shows the first four bars of "Blue Bossa" with both minor 7th chords changed to minor 6th chords.

Ex. 2-13   "Blue Bossa" using Bebop Melodic Minor Scales in Drop-2

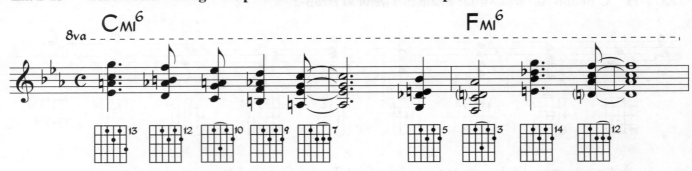

Another option for a tonic minor chord is to play it as a minor-major chord, which has a minor 3rd and major 7th, as shown in the tweaked (it has a 9th) C minor-major chord in Ex. 2-14 (CD1 Track #40).

Ex. 2-14

Now play Ex. 2-15 (CD1 Track #41). The first chord in "Blue Bossa" is now a minor-major chord, and the diminished chords are tweaked.

Ex. 2-15   "Blue Bossa" using Tweaked Drop-2 voicings

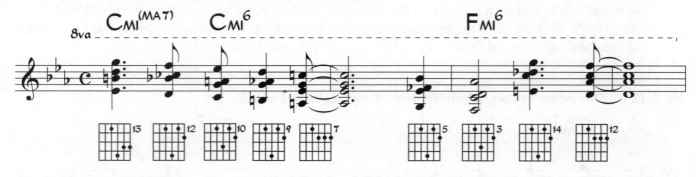

Play Ex. 2-15 a few times, and then go back and play Ex. 2-12. Which do you like best? Ex.2-15 is certainly much more radical than Ex. 2-12. If it's too far out for you, you don't have to tweak everything. By the way, Ex. 2-12 and Ex. 2-15 are the same as the first two examples at the beginning of the book, Ex. 1-1 and Ex. 1-2.

Now let's check out how we tweak the tonic minor chords. Ex. 2-16 (CD1 Track #42) shows all four Cm6 chords in standard drop 2 from chapter 1, plus their tweaked counterparts. For now we are not going to tweak the Cm6 with the note C, the root, in the melody (Ex. 2-16a). It's somewhat problematic, but you can find a tweaked version in the appendix. At any rate, the original sounds fine as it is. In Ex. 2-16b we raise the note A, the 6th, a whole step to the note B, the major 7th, creating a CmMaj7 chord. In Ex. 2-16c we raise two notes, A, the 6th, and C, the root, by whole steps to B, the major 7th, and D, the 9th, forming a CmMaj9 chord. In Ex. 2-16d the note C, the root, is raised a whole step to D, the 9th, forming a Cm6/9 chord.

Ex. 2-16   Tweaking tonic minor chords

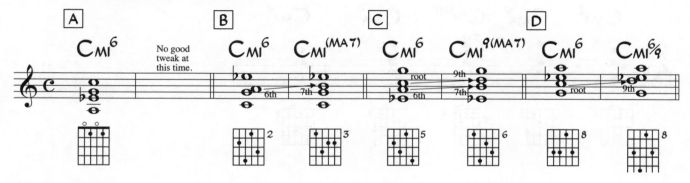

Now play Ex. 2-17 (CD1 Track #43), the C Bebop Melodic Minor Scale in tweaked drop 2.

Ex. 2-17   C Bebop Melodic Minor Scale in Tweaked Drop-2

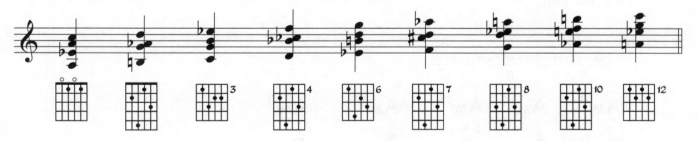

The tweaked C tonic minor chords are all from Ex. 2-16, while the tweaked diminished chords are from Ex. 2-2A. Compare with Ex. 2-18 (CD1 Track #44), the same C Bebop Melodic Minor Scale using the same tweaked minor chords combined with the tweaked diminished chords from Ex. 2-2B.

Ex. 2-18   C Bebop Melodic Minor Scale in Tweaked Drop-2

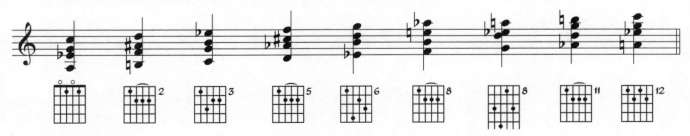

Also compare these with the standard drop 2 from chapter 1 and experiment with a variety of combinations.

Tweaking Extension Voicings

While we're at it, we might as well tweak the voicings for melody notes that are treated as chord extensions that were given in chapter 1. Ex. 2-19 (CD1 Track #45) shows tweaked voicings for the major chord extensions major 7th, 9th, and #11th.

Ex. 2-19

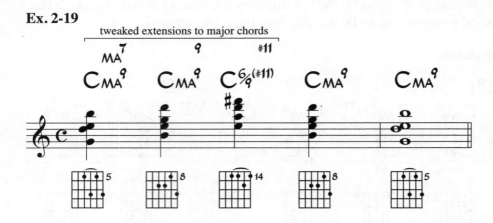

Ex. 2-20 (CD1 Track #46) shows the tweaked voicings for the minor 7 chord extensions 9th, 11th, and 13th.

Ex. 2-20

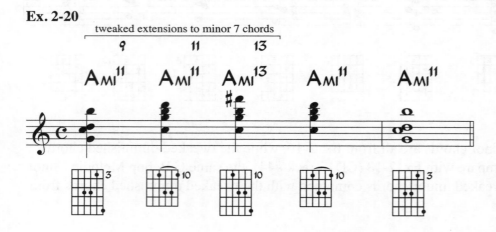

Ex. 2-21 (CD1 Track #47) shows the tweaked voicings for the tonic minor chord extensions major 7th, 9th, and 11th.

Ex. 2-21

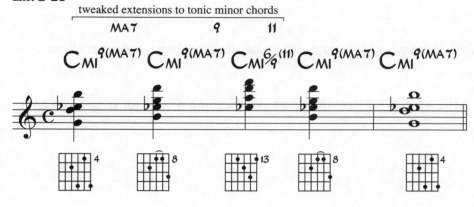

Ex. 2-22 (CD1 Track #48) shows the tweaked voicings for the dominant 7 chord extensions 9th, #11th, and 13th.

Ex. 2-22

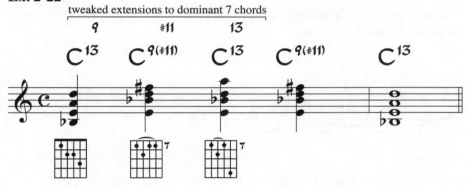

By now you should be able to understand how this was done. You can find alternate variations in the appendix.

CHAPTER 3 - SOLOING AND COMPING IN DROP 2

Enclosures

Enclosure means to precede a note with two other notes, one slightly above, the other slightly below.

Play Ex. 3-1 (CD1 Track #49), a simple descending melody outlining a C major triad containing the four notes E, C, G, E.

Ex. 3-1

In Ex. 3-2 (CD1 Track #50) each melody note - E, C, G, E - is enclosed by two notes, one above the melody note and one below. These two notes can be either a half step or a whole step above or below the melody note, but in this type of enclosure *they must be a minor 3rd apart from each other, making them from the same diminished chord.*

Ex. 3-2

The first melody note in Ex. 3-1 is E. I'm preceding it with F, the note a half step above it. F's diminished chord is (reading down) F, D, B, and Ab. The next enclosure note will be D, a minor 3rd down from the first note, and from the same diminished chord.

I take a similar approach on the other melody notes from Ex. 3-1, except I'm starting the enclosures of C and G from a whole step above, so C is enclosed by D and B, while the G is enclosed by A and F#.

Example 3-3 (CD1 Track #51) shows Ex. 3-2 played in drop 2.

Ex. 3-3

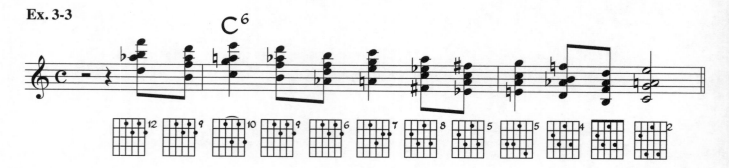

Ex. 3-4 (CD1 Track #52) encloses almost the same melody as in Ex. 3-1, but over a Cm6 chord. The notes enclosing the melody are from the same diminished chord - F, D, B, Ab.

Ex. 3-4

Ex. 3-5 (CD1 Track #53) shows Ex. 3-4 in drop 2.

Ex. 3-5

Chromatic Approach Chords

Play Ex. 3-6 (CD1 Track #54), an excerpt from "How High The Moon" as recorded by Joe Pass on his famous solo guitar recording *Virtuoso*.

Ex. 3-6   "How High The Moon" from Joe Pass' version

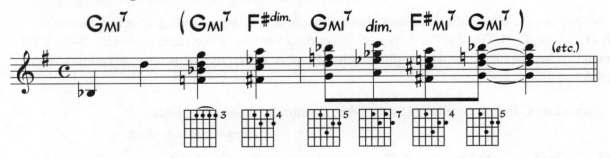

The drop 2 block chord passage (no pun intended) is really all just a Gm7, but Joe uses the G bebop natural minor scale in drop 2 combined with a form of enclosure that uses a *chromatic approach chord*, the F#m7. It harmonizes the note A, which is a half step below the chord tone Bb, the minor 3rd of the Gm7. Any chord can be approached by the same type of chord from a half step below or above if it harmonizes a melody note a half step below or above a chord tone of the target chord. Remember, the melody may be the melody of a tune, or part of an improvised solo line, or a background melody used for comping behind another musician's melody or improvised solo.

Ex. 3-7 (CD1 Track #55) shows a modified version of the enclosure melody in drop 2 from Ex. 3-3. This time all the lower notes of the enclosures are always a half step below the chord tones, even if they don't belong to the diminished chord of the upper note, so as to be harmonized with chromatic approach chords.

Ex. 3-7

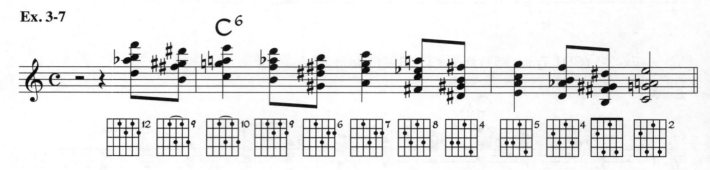

Ex. 3-8 (CD1 Track #56) shows the same concept applied to the enclosure melody in drop 2 from Ex. 3-4.

Ex. 3-8

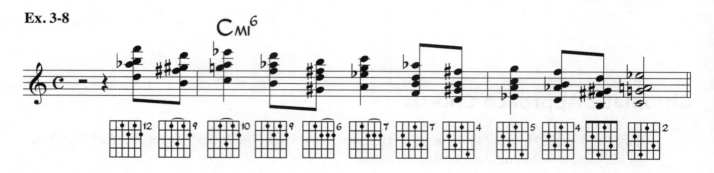

Ex. 3-9 applies the chromatic approach chord concept first to an ascending C bebop dominant scale (Ex. 3-9a, CD1 Track #57), then to a descending version of the same scale (Ex. 3-9b, CD1 Track #58). Notice the chromatic approach chords are in different places when ascending than when descending.

Ex. 3-09a   Ascending C Bebop Dominant Scale using chromatic approach chords

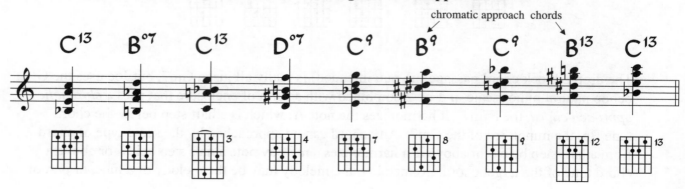

Ex. 3-09b Descending C Bebop Dominant Scale using chromatic approach chords

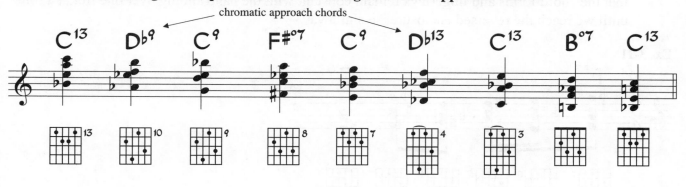

Try applying this same concept to the bebop major, bebop natural minor, and bebop melodic minor scales as well.

Chromatic approach chords lie easily on guitar and lend themselves to slurring since the hand slides an identical chord form up or down by one fret. Try slurring the approach chords on all the above examples by sliding the left hand without re-striking the strings with the right hand. Pretty cool, huh? Welcome to the realm of Wes, Benson and Pass.

Elaborated Enclosures

The same feature of the guitar that allows slurring by sliding also allows for some amazing *elaborated enclosures*, enclosures with chromatic "fill-ins", that, although easy on guitar, would be quite challenging on piano. These will be based on melodic embellishments that bebop master Barry Harris calls "surrounding the notes of the major 6 and minor 6 chords". They use a chromatic fragment that connects one note of a passing diminished chord to the next note of the same chord, then enclosing and resolving to the target note in the major 6 or minor 6 chord. We'll start by checking out the major 6 chord first.

Play Ex. 3-10 (CD1 Track #59). This melody outlines a C6 chord using elaborated enclosures that begin above each target chord tone and use a descending chromatic fragment followed by a reversed enclosure (starting below, then above, the target chord note).

Ex. 3-10

Ex. 3-11 (CD1 Track #60) shows the drop 2 harmonization of the fourth bar of Ex. 3-10. Notice that the chord forms and fingerings remain constant with the hand sliding over one fret at a time until we reach the reversed enclosure, so slur away.

Ex. 3-11

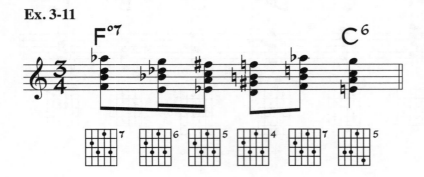

Now work out the drop 2 voicings for the rest of Ex. 3-10 (CD1 Track #61). If you've been working through this book this should be easy to do by now.

Ex. 3-12 (CD1 Track #62) reverses the order, starting below each C6 chord note and ascending chromatically until we reach a standard enclosure.

Ex. 3-12

Ex. 3-13 (CD1 Track #63) shows the drop 2 voicings for the fourth measure of Ex. 3-12. Be sure to work out the rest of Ex. 3-12 in drop 2 (CD1 Track #64).

Ex. 3-13

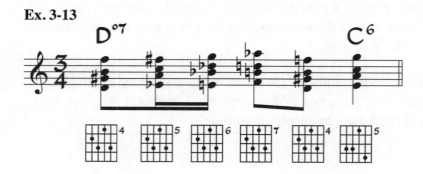

Ex. 3-14 (CD1 Track #65) is almost identical to Ex. 3-12, except the last note before each C6 chord note is always a half step below it's target to facilitate harmonization with chromatic approach chords.

Ex. 3-14

Ex. 3-15 (CD1 Track #66) shows the fourth bar of Ex. 3-14 in drop 2 with a chromatic approach chord (the B6). Work out the rest of Ex. 3-14 in drop 2 using B6 chromatic approach chords (CD1 Track #67).

Ex. 3-15

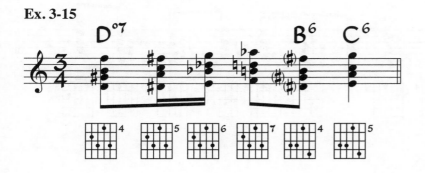

Now go back through the previous examples, but change all the target chord E notes to Eb, creating elaborated enclosures of the Cm6 chord (CD1 Track #68 and #69). When working the example using chromatic approach chords, all the B6 chords must be changed to Bm6 chords by lowering all the D# notes to D natural (CD1 Track #70).

Ex. 3-16 (CD1 Track #71) shows the first four bars of Jerome Kern's "All The Things You Are".

Ex. 3-16   Jerome Kern's "All The Things You Are"

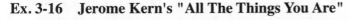

We're going to solo over this using drop 2. Jazz musicians seldom play the exact changes notated. We like to reharmonize as we go along to make the song more interesting. The third measure of the example has already been reharmonized with a common form of reharmonization called *tritone substitution*. The original harmony was just Eb7 for the whole bar. We've replaced it with Em7 to A7, the II-V progression borrowed from the key of D, which is a tritone away from our home key of Ab (hence the name "tritone substitution").

Ex. 3-17 (CD1 Track #72) is a solo line on the first four bars of "All The Things You Are" in drop 2. In addition to the tritone substitution, all the minor 7 chords have been changed to minor 6 chords.

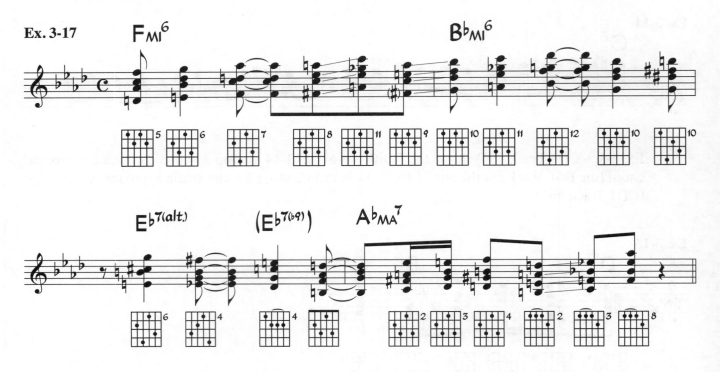

Ex. 3-17 uses several techniques:

In bar #1:

1) The original Fm7 chord has been reharmonized as Fm6.

2) An improvised melody ascends the first three notes of the F bebop melodic minor scale in drop 2.

3) The fourth and fifth chords in the bar are the same diminished chord, but not from the F bebop minor scale indicated by the chord symbol Fm6. It is a transitional chord, a dominant 7th chord inserted to flow smoothly into Bbm6, the following chord. Its four notes - A, C, Eb and F# - are the 3rd, 5th, 7th and b9th of F7b9, the dominant chord that resolves to the next chord, Bbm6.

4) The diminished chords are part of an enclosure that uses a chromatic approach chord. The last chord in the measure is Am6, a chromatic approach chord to Bbm6, the first chord in the second bar.

In bar #2:

1) The original Bbm7 chord has been reharmonized as Bbm6.

2) An improvised melody ascends the first three notes of the Bb bebop melodic minor scale in drop 2.

In bar #3:

   1) The second and third chords are from the altered bebop minor scale, which we'll look at next.

In bar #4:

   1) The first five chords form an elaborated enclosure, as in Ex. 3-15, that uses a chromatic approach chord. The 5th of the Ab major chord is harmonized by a fourth chord (an alternate tweak - see the appendix), so the chromatic approach chord is likewise a fourth chord, G6/9.

The Altered Bebop Minor Scale

Ex. 3-18 (CD1 Track #73) shows the C altered bebop minor scale. This scale is different from the other scales you have studied because it doesn't routinely alternate a chord (major, minor, or dominant) with a diminished chord. The actual melody notes of the scale are identical to the C bebop natural minor scale, but with significantly different harmonies. Most of the scale is harmonized as if it were a C bebop melodic minor scale, but the natural minor note Bb is voiced with a chord that is labeled, somewhat arbitrarily, G7alt. Remember that the diminished chords in the scale represent G7b9, so we now have three G7 chords in a row, creating new possibilities.

Ex. 3-18   C Altered Bebop Minor Scale

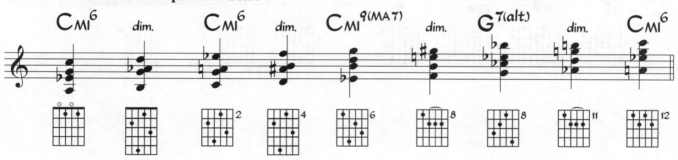

Counting from the beginning of Ex. 3-18, look at the sixth and seventh chords in the bar, labeled "dim" and "G7alt". Since the diminished chord is really G7b9, we can use the voicing pair moving in minor 3rds to harmonize a diminished scale melody. Let's start down a tritone to give us more room to move the voicings up the scale (Ex. 3-19, CD1 Track #74).

Ex. 3-19   Two chords ascending in minor 3rds

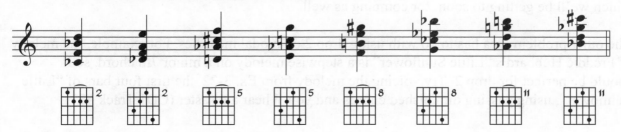

Many improvised lines follow this whole-step/half-step pattern. Ex. 3-20 (CD1 Track #75) shows the line over a *minor II-V progression*.

Ex. 3-20

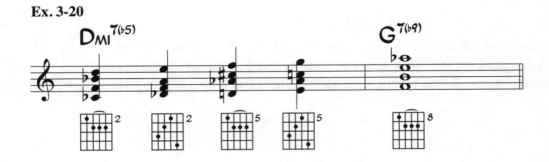

Ex. 3-21 (CD1 Track #76) shows how the minor II-V progression might go on to resolve to a C minor, using an extension voicing (tweaked) to harmonize the B natural melody note as CmMaj9.

Ex. 3-21

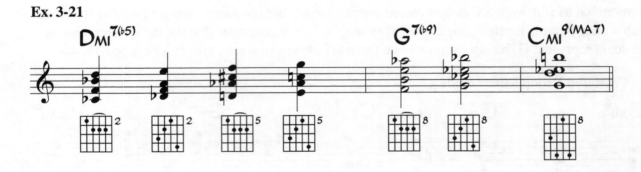

Problems with Drop 2

A word of caution about playing drop 2 while comping behind another musician's solo: If you play too many passing diminished chords or too many enclosures, you run the risk of creating some serious clashes with the soloist, which could result in another guitarist or pianist getting called for the next gig! It's usually safe to use the basic and tweaked chord tone voicings as well as the basic and tweaked extension voicings. It's frequently OK to use modal drop 2 voicings, which we'll be getting to soon, for comping as well.

The other problem area has to do with using drop 2 on modal melodies. For example, the melody of Freddie Hubbard's "Little Sunflower" is a stepwise melody on a minor 7th chord, so it should be perfect for drop 2. Try voicing the melody from Ex. 3-22, the first four bars of "Little Sunflower", using passing diminished chords and you'll hear a disaster (CD1 Track #77).

Ex. 3-22 Freddie Hubbard's "Little Sunflower"

We'll find a great solution to this problem in the section on modal drop 2 voicings, but first let's look at some comp voicings in drop 2 for II-V- I.

II-V-I Comp Lines in Drop 2

Let's explore a concept for developing some really useful II-V-I comp voicings forming simple background lines. We want the lines to be good melodies without being so complex as to get in the way of the soloist you're accompanying. On a II-V-I in C major, let's have each chord last for one measure, and let's have only two melody notes on the II chord and on the V chord and one resolution note on the I chord, making a five note melody line that we can harmonize in drop 2. For now we'll just use half and whole notes to learn the voicings, and we'll avoid passing diminished chords and enclosures, although we may dip into a few alternate voicings from the appendix.

Ex. 3-23

To start we'll compose a simple five note melody starting from each note of a Dm11 chord, the root, D, the 3rd, F, the 5th, A, the 7th, C, the 9th, E, and the 11th, G. Ex. 3-23 (CD1 Track #78) is a collection of possible melodies, although there are many more waiting to be discovered.
The first three II-V-I lines are simple diatonic melodies that fit nicely into the chord changes. The last three each have one chromatic note, the Eb in the fourth line, functioning as the b13 of G7, the Ab in the fifth line, functioning as the b9 of G7, and the C# in the sixth line, functioning as the #11 of G7. Notice all the chromatic notes are on the V chord. This is because the dominant7th chord accepts many altered notes as harmonic extensions, while major and minor7th chords generally don't.

Ex. 3-24 (CD1 Track #79) shows a drop 2 harmonization of the first line from Ex. 3-23, starting on the root of the Dm7 chord. The first voicing is basic drop 2, the second and third are tweaked, and the fourth reharmonizes the F note as the 3rd of Db7, the tritone substitution for G7 (the Db7 is also tweaked).

Ex. 3-24

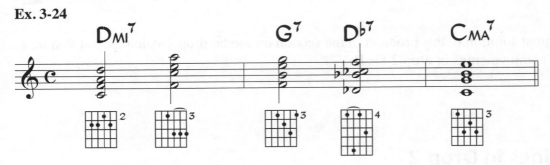

Ex. 3-25 (CD1 Track #80) shows the second line from Ex. 3-23 (starting on the 3rd of the Dm7) in drop 2. All the voicings in the example are tweaked. The B note on the G7 is reharmonized as the 7th of Db9, while the G note (the root) on the G7 is reharmonized as the #11 (extension voicing) of Db9#11, a much more interesting note than the root.

Ex. 3-25

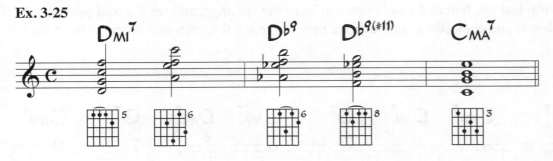

Ex. 3-26 (CD1 Track #81) shows the third line from Ex. 3-23 (starting on the 5th of Dm7) voiced in drop 2. The first two voicings are tweaked, while the third and fourth use something new, diminished voicings representing G7b9 as an actual dominant chord rather than as a passing chord. The first one is tweaked, while the second is basic. The C major chord is an alternate

Ex. 3-26

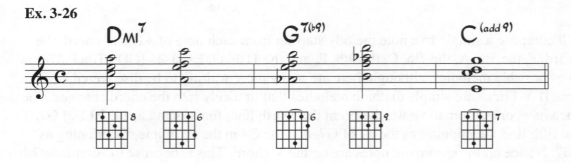

tweak (see appendix), Cadd9 for C6.

Ex. 3-27 (CD1 Track #82) is a drop 2 harmonization of the fourth line from Ex. 3-23, starting on the 7th of Dm7. The first Dm7 voicing is tweaked, the second is a tweaked extension voicing harmonizing the 9th. The b13 on the G7 uses a basic Db7 extension voicing (the Eb is the b13 of G7, but is the 9th of Db7), while the 3rd is reharmonized as the 7th of a tweaked Db7. The Cmajor is a tweaked extension voicing harmonizing the 9th.

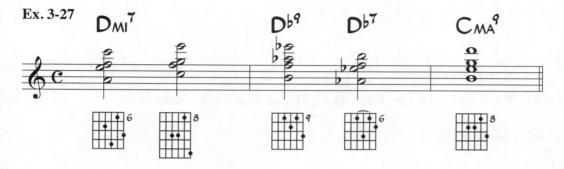

Ex. 3-28 (CD1 Track #83) shows a possible drop 2 version of the fifth line from Ex. 3-23, starting on the 9th of Dm7. The first voicing is the tweaked extension voicing for the 9th. The G7 voicings are once again using diminished chords for G7b9. The first is tweaked by raising the third note from the top by a whole step; the second is tweaked by raising the second note from the top by a whole step. The last chord is an alternate tweak (see appendix), a fourth chord forming a C6/9.

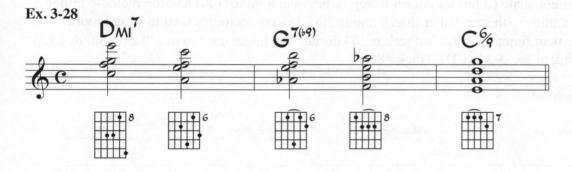

Ex. 3-29 (CD1 Track #84) shows the last line from Ex. 3-23 in drop 2, starting on the 11th of Dm7. The first voicing is an alternate tweaked extension voicing. The #11 on the G7 is voiced with a tweaked extension voicing; the 5th uses a basic diminished chord for G7b9.

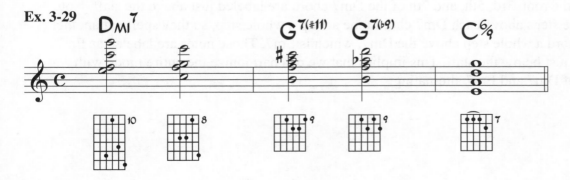

Of course none of these examples show us any decent comping rhythms or punctuation but that's a subject for another book. These are to demonstrate how to use slow moving melodies to select good voicings for your comping.

Modal Drop 2

Play Ex. 3-30 (CD1 Track #85), the first three bars of Duke Pearson's "Jeannine".

Ex. 3-30   Duke Pearson's "Jeannine"

If you try to voice it in drop 2 using diminished chords to harmonize the non chord tones (the F's), it just doesn't work (similar to the "Little Sunflower" example earlier). The melodies of both "Jeannine" and of "Little Sunflower" are written in the Dorian mode, which differs from the natural minor scale (it has a major 6th step rather than a minor 6th) and the melodic minor scale (it has a minor 7th step rather than a major 7th). Dorian melodies tend to sound more *modal* rather than functional. Let's check out D dorian, the mode used in our "Little Sunflower" example. Look at Ex. 3-31 (CD1 Track #86).

Ex. 3-31   D Dorian Mode

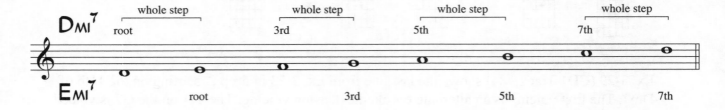

Notice that the root, 3rd, 5th, and 7th of the Dm7 chord are labeled just above the staff. Note that the scale steps above each Dm7 chord tone are up a whole step, so they spell out another minor7th chord a whole step above the Dm7, which is Em7. Those notes are labeled as Em7 chord tones just below the staff. This implies that we can harmonize the entire mode with inversions of Dm7 and Em7 alternating.

Now let's try Ex. 3-32 (CD1 Track #87), D dorian in modal drop 2.

Ex. 3-32   D Dorian in Modal Drop-2

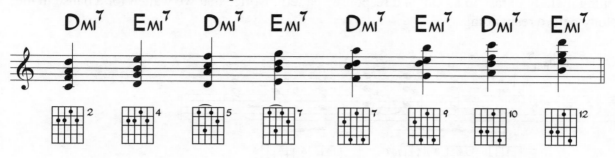

That works very well. Let's see if we can apply this concept to "Little Sunflower". Play Ex. 3-33 (CD1 Track #88).

Ex. 3-33   "Little Sunflower" in Modal Drop-2

Now we have a satisfactory result. The entire fragment is harmonized using only basic Dm7 and Em7 voicings. Some notes may have more than one choice. For example, the D note at the end of the third bar is the root of Dm7 and the 7th of Em7. We could have voiced it as Em7 and the high E in the fourth bar with an extension voicing (Dm9). Give it a try (CD1 Track #89).

Now let's return to "Jeannine". Play Ex. 3-34 (CD1 Track #90), the first three bars of "Jeannine" in modal drop 2.

Ex. 3-34   "Jeannine" in Modal Drop-2

Now let's try something new, a comp figure using modal drop 2. Ex. 3-35 (CD1 Track #91) is a phrase to accompany the melody of "Jeannine". It begins in the third measure and answers the opening melody phrase in a "call and response" pattern. Notice that we waited for a pause in the melody before responding.

Ex. 3-35

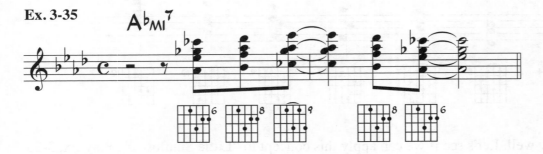

These dorian modal drop 2 voicings can be used for other modes as well. For example, the most common uses for D dorian would be for F Lydian mode (remember, F6=Dm7) and for G Mixolydian mode (Dm7/G=G7sus).

A very interesting mode for D half-diminished is *D locrian #2,* the sixth mode of melodic minor. Look at Ex. 3-36 (CD1 Track #92).

Ex. 3-36   D Locrian #2 Mode

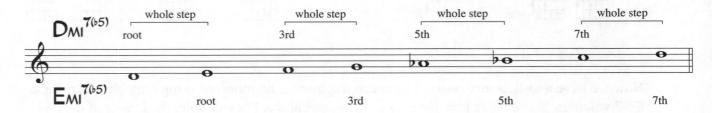

The root, 3rd, 5th and 7th of D half-diminished (Dm7b5) are labeled just above the staff. Notice that, once again, the scale steps above each Dm7b5 chord tone are all up a whole step, spelling out an Em7b5 chord. Those notes are labeled as E half-diminished chord tones just below the staff. We can harmonize the entire mode by alternating Dm7b5 and Em7b5 voicings.

Ex. 3-37 (CD1 Track #93) shows D locrian #2 in modal drop 2.

Ex. 3-37   D Locrian #2 in Modal Drop-2

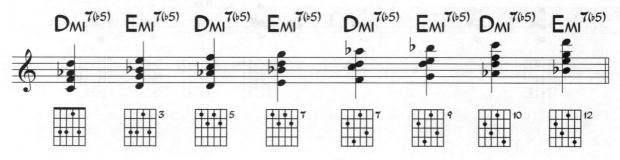

You might be wondering how often a melody is in locrian #2. Well, it's very rare, but, being a mode of the melodic minor scale, it has broad applications over many other modes and chords. For example, Dm7b5 has the same notes as Fm6. Let's return to our previously promised modal drop 2 harmonization of "Summertime" (Ex. 3-38, CD1 Track #94). It's in A minor, so we'll use F# locrian #2 (Am6=F#m7b5).

Ex. 3-38   George Gershwin's "Summertime" in Modal Drop-2

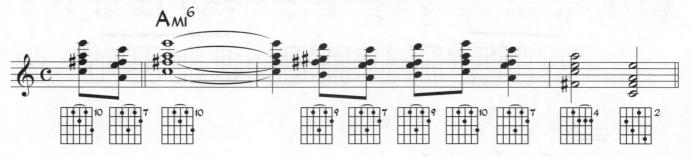

This time we voiced the entire fragment with F#m7b5 and G#m7b5 chords, or more accurately in this case, Am6 and Bm6 chords (as did George Gershwin, by the way).

Some other applications of D locrian #2 include Bb Lydian Dominant (Dm9b5/Bb=Bb9#11), E Altered Dominant (Dm7b5/E=E7#5b9), and G phrygian #6 (Dm9b5/G=G13susb9).

We'll look at one more fragment, then we'll be done and can move on to how to practice drop 2. Ex. 3-39 (CD1 Track #95) is the first three bars of the bridge of Arthur Hamilton's "Cry Me A River" in standard drop 2.

Ex. 3-39   Arthur Hamilton's "Cry Me A River" in Standard Drop-2

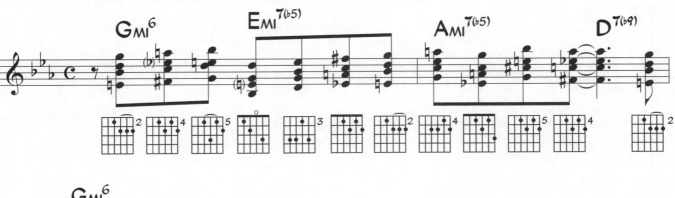

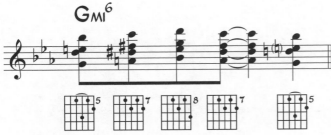

Ex. 3-40 (CD1 Track #96) shows the same three bars using modal drop 2.

Ex. 3-40   "Cry Me A River" in Modal Drop-2

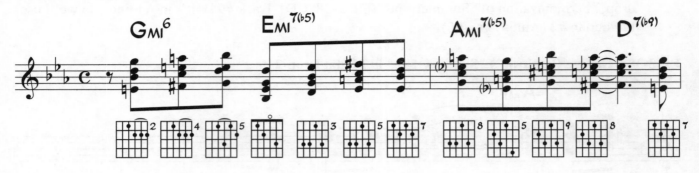

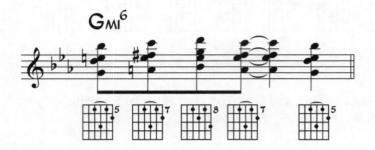

Obviously either way works in this case. You may prefer parts of one and other parts of the other, so mix as you see fit. At any rate, with standard voicings, extension voicings, tweaked voicings, chromatic approach chords and modal voicings you have enough choices to find whatever solution you feel is best for any given situation.

CHAPTER 4 - PRACTICING DROP 2

Practicing drop 2 can be a challenge. While many of the voicings may be familiar and/or easy, many of the tweaked and extension voicings may be new and unfamiliar (and some are physically demanding), and the combinations involved are a real workout. In order to use the material in this book successfully, you will need a practice routine. What follows are some suggestions as to what you should be practicing.

Unlike the piano, the guitar does not require different hand-keyboard shapes for every key, but the hand-fingerboard shapes are different on different sets of strings, so we need to practice each new key on all three sets of four consecutive strings (remember, drop 2 voicings cover four consecutive strings on guitar). Eventually you should cover every key on all the sets of strings by going around the circle of keys, but after the first few you'll start to see how the same shapes work in every key.

The lowest four strings (3rd through 6th) tend to sound "muddy" and are impractical for physical and sonic reasons to use to play tweaked voicings. About 95% or more of our drop 2 work will be on the top two sets (1st through 4th and 2nd through 5th), but we will check out the standard drop 2 voicings on every set.

Bebop Scales

Play Ex. 4-1 (CD2 - Track #1, it's the same as Ex. 1-6 from the first chapter).

Ex. 4-1   C Bebop Major Scale on middle strings

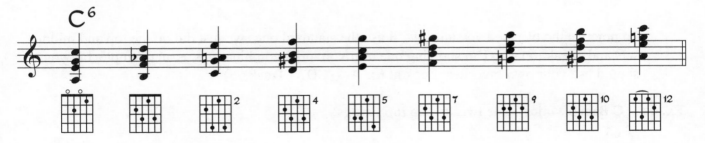

This is one octave of the C bebop major scale on the middle set of strings. It so happens that the lowest practical drop 2 chord tone voicing on this set is the root, so we go root up to root. What the example doesn't show is the fact that we also must play the scale descending (CD2 - Track #2) from the high C back down to the bottom (step-wise melodies don't always ascend - they also frequently descend). Now we need to practice these same voicings in this same key on the top four strings (when I say "top four" I mean the highest in pitch, not the closest to the ceiling!).

Ex. 4-2 shows how this is done.

Ex. 4-2   C Bebop Major Scale on top strings

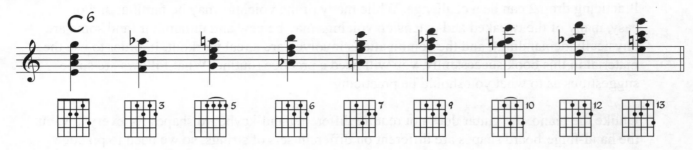

Notice that we start with the lowest practical chord tone voicing in the key of C on this set of strings, the note G, and go up the scale one octave to the next highest G (remember to descend the scale from the high G back down to where we started, CD2 - Track #3).

Ex. 4-3 shows how we do the C bebop major scale in drop 2 on the bottom set of four strings.

Ex. 4-3   C Bebop Major Scale on bottom strings

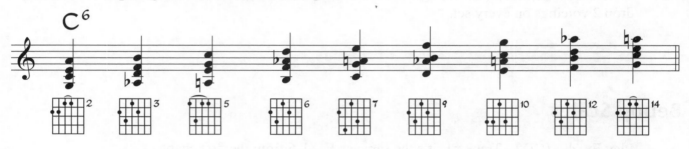

Practice the scale ascending and descending (CD2 - Track #4).

To practice the tweaked versions, we'll use the standard ones we just did on the top and middle sets and tweak to taste. I'm showing one of my favorite combinations as an example, but you should use your own favorites. Look at Ex. 4-4 (CD2 - Track #5).

Ex. 4-4   C Bebop Major Scale tweaked on top strings

This is the tweaked scale on the top set. Notice I used different tweaked diminished chords in different parts of the scale (that's what sounded good to me). Ex. 4-5 (CD2 - Track #6) shows the same tweaks on the middle set.

Ex. 4-5   C Bebop Major Scale tweaked on middle strings

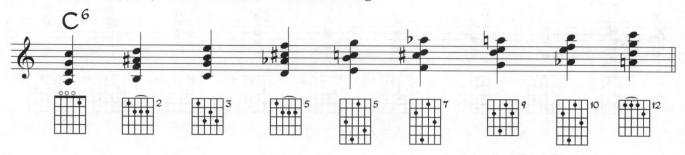

The next step would be to do it in the key of F. I'll start on the middle set since we started there in C. The lowest note in C that had a playable voicing was C, but the voicing for the C note in the F bebop major scale is not playable there, so let's start with the D, the next chord tone up (these are the type of adjustments you'll have to make as you go through the keys). Play Ex. 4-6 (CD2 - Track #7), the F bebop major scale in standard drop 2 on the middle set of four consecutive strings.

Ex. 4-6   F Bebop Major Scale on middle strings

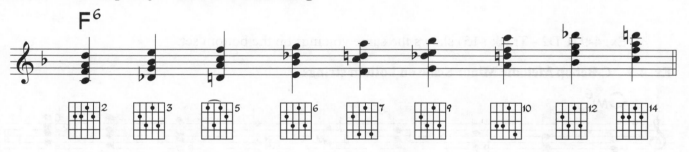

Now take this through the same process that we did in the key of C: first, work out the standard drop 2 voicings in F on the top set of four (CD2 - Track #8) and the bottom set of four strings (CD2 - Track #9), then do tweaked drop 2 on the top (CD2 - Track #10) and middle sets (CD2 - Track #11). Remember to practice both ascending and descending.

It's also a good idea to try a long full range scale using all the string sets. For example, in the key of C, start on the bottom set and play the voicings for the notes A, B, C, D, and E, then switch to the middle set for the notes F, G, G# (or Ab), A, and B, and then on to the top set for the notes C, D, E, F, and G, and finally descend in reverse order (CD2 - Track #12).

Ex. 4-7 (CD2 - Track #13) shows the C bebop melodic minor scale in standard drop 2 on the middle set of four consecutive strings (it's the same as Ex. 1-12 from Chapter 1).

Ex. 4-7 C Bebop Melodic Minor Scale on middle strings

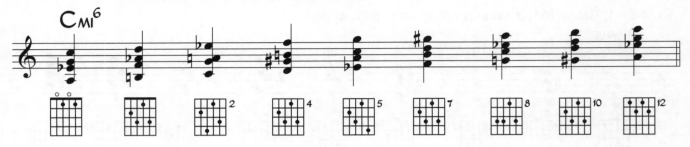

Ex. 4-8 (CD2 - Track #14) shows the same voicings on the top set.

Ex. 4-8 C Bebop Melodic Minor Scale on top strings

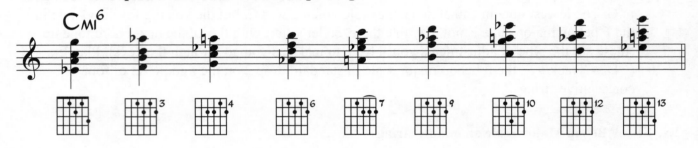

Ex. 4-9 (CD2 - Track #15) shows the same voicings on the bottom set.

Ex. 4-9 C Bebop Melodic Minor Scale on bottom strings

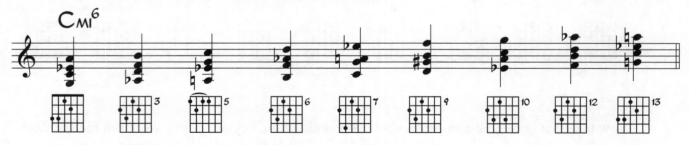

Ex. 4-10 (CD2 - Track #16) shows the tweaked C bebop melodic minor scale on the middle set of four consecutive strings.

Ex. 4-10 C Bebop Melodic Minor Scale tweaked on middle strings

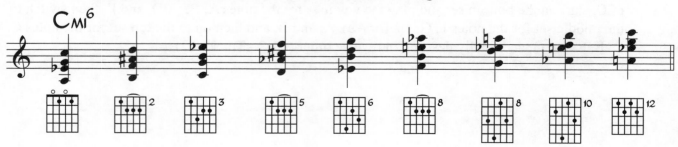

Ex. 4-11 (CD2 - Track #17) shows the same voicings on the top set.

Ex. 4-11 C Bebop Melodic Minor Scale tweaked on top strings

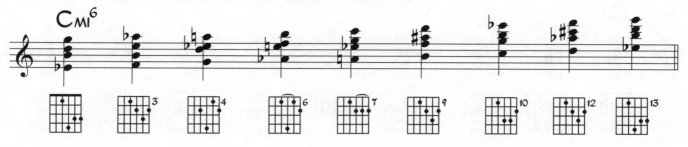

Remember to practice all the scales both ascending and descending, and eventually in every key.

Ex. 4-12 (CD2 - Track #18) shows the C bebop dominant scale in standard drop 2 on the middle set of four consecutive strings (it's the same as Ex. 1-14 from Chapter 1).

Ex. 4-12 C Bebop Dominant Scale on middle strings

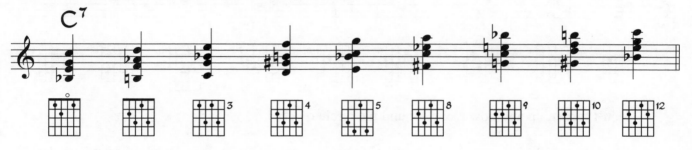

Ex. 4-13 (CD2 - Track #19) shows the same voicings on the top set.

Ex. 4-13 C Bebop Dominant Scale on top strings

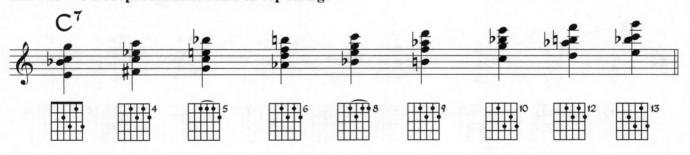

Ex. 4-14 (CD2 - Track #20) shows them on the bottom set.

Ex. 4-14 C Bebop Dominant Scale on bottom strings

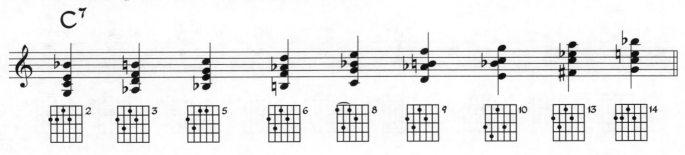

Ex. 4-15 (CD2 - Track #21) shows the tweaked voicings on the middle set.

Ex. 4-15   C Bebop Dominant Scale tweaked on middle strings

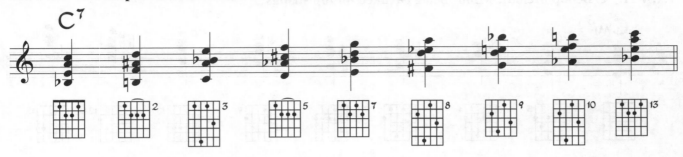

Ex. 4-16 (CD2 - Track #22) shows the tweaked voicings on the top set.

Ex. 4-16   C Bebop Dominant Scale tweaked on top strings

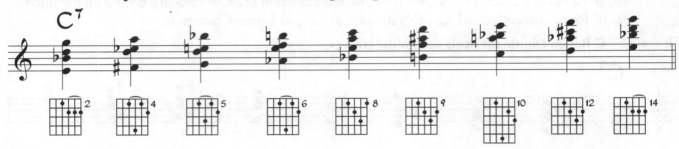

Don't forget, up and down, and around the circle of keys.

Ex. 4-17 (CD2 - Track #23) shows the C bebop natural minor scale in standard drop 2 on the middle set of four consecutive strings.

Ex. 4-17   C Bebop Natural Minor Scale on middle strings

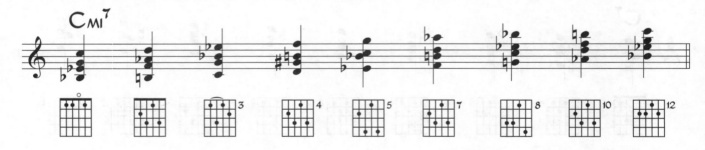

Ex. 4-18 (CD2 - Track #24) shows the same voicings on the top set.

Ex. 4-18   C Bebop Natural Minor Scale on top strings

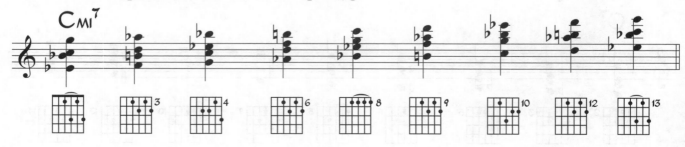

Ex. 4-19 (CD2 - Track #25) shows them on the bottom set.

Ex. 4-19   C Bebop Natural Minor Scale on bottom strings

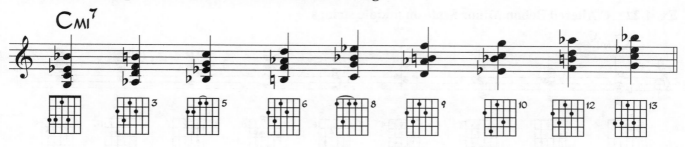

Ex. 4-20 (CD2 - Track #26) shows the tweaked voicings on the middle set.

Ex. 4-20   C Bebop Natural Minor Scale tweaked on middle strings

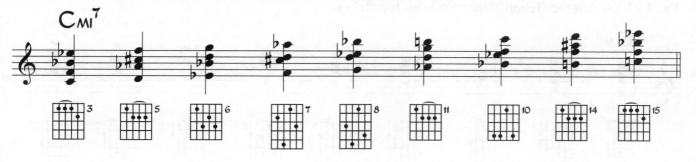

Ex. 4-21 (CD2 - Track #27) shows the tweaked voicings on the top set.

Ex. 4-21   C Bebop Natural Minor Scale tweaked on top strings

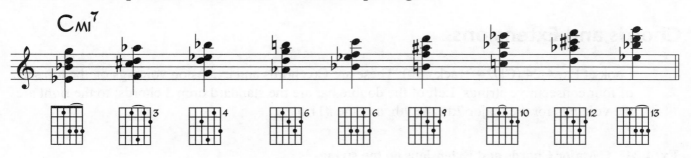

Remember to descend as well as ascend, and go around the cycle into other keys, eventually covering all keys.

Ex. 4-22 (CD2 - Track #28) shows the C altered bebop minor scale in drop 2 on the middle set of four consecutive strings.

Ex. 4-22   C Altered Bebop Minor Scale on middle strings

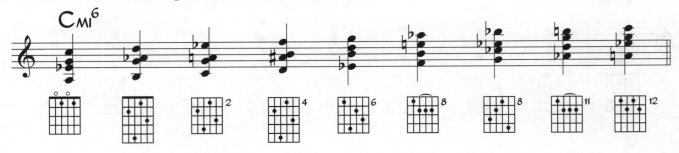

Ex. 4-23 (CD2 - Track #29) shows the same voicings on the top set.

Ex. 4-23   C Altered Bebop Minor Scale on top strings

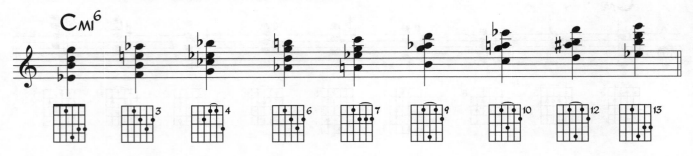

Chords and Extensions

Look at Ex. 4-24 (CD2 - Track #30). These are C6 chords and extension voicings on the top set of four consecutive strings. Left of the double bar are the standard drop 2 chords; to the right are the voicings for the major 7th, the 9th, and the #11th.

Ex. 4-24   C Major Chords and Extensions on top strings

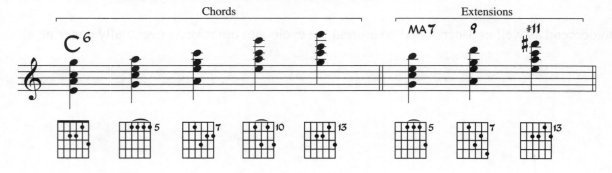

Ex. 4-25 (CD2 - Track #31) shows the same voicings on the middle set.

Ex. 4-25   C Major Chords and Extensions on middle strings

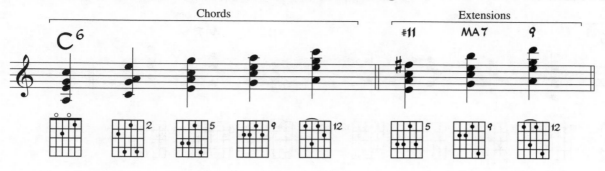

Ex. 4-26 (CD2 - Track #32) shows them on the bottom set.

Ex. 4-26   C Major Chords and Extensions on bottom strings

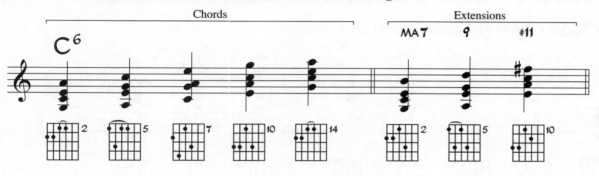

Ex. 4-27 (CD2 - Track #33) shows the tweaked major chords and extensions on the top set.

Ex. 4-27   Tweaked C Major Chords and Extensions on top strings

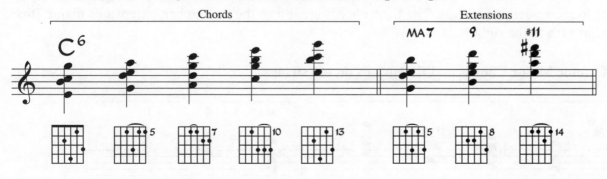

Ex. 4-28 (CD2 - Track #34) shows them on the middle set.

Ex. 4-28   Tweaked C Major Chords and Extensions on middle strings

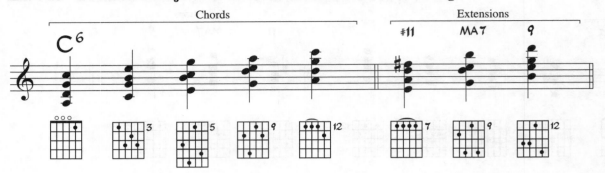

Like the bebop scales, these should be played ascending and descending, and taken through the cycle of keys. Ex. 4-29 (CD2 - Track #35) shows example 4-24 transposed into the key of F major as a model. The other keys are up to you to work out. By the time you've gone through four or five keys, you'll know one heck of a lot about the guitar and about harmony.

Ex. 4-29   F Major Chords and Extensions on top strings

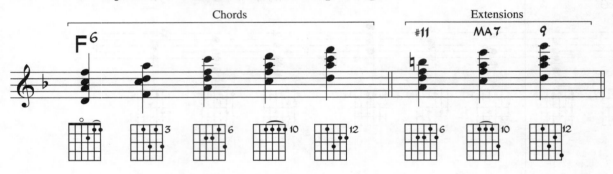

Ex. 4-30 (CD2 - Track #36) shows the C tonic minor chords and extension voicings on the top set of four consecutive strings. The Cm6 chords are left of the double bar, extensions major 7th, 9th, and 11th to the right.

Ex. 4-30   C Tonic Minor Chords and Extensions on top strings

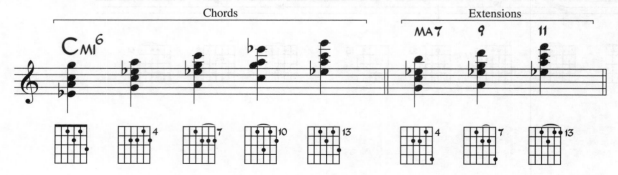

Ex. 4-31 (CD2 - Track #37) shows the same voicings on the middle set.

Ex. 4-31   C Tonic Minor Chords and Extensions on middle strings

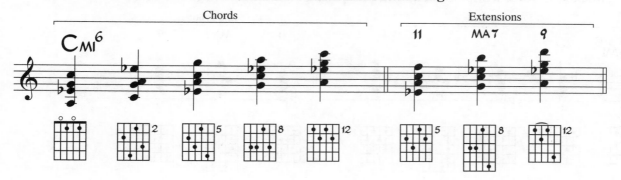

Ex. 4-32 (CD2 - Track #38) shows them on the bottom set.

Ex. 4-32   C Tonic Minor Chords and Extensions on bottom strings

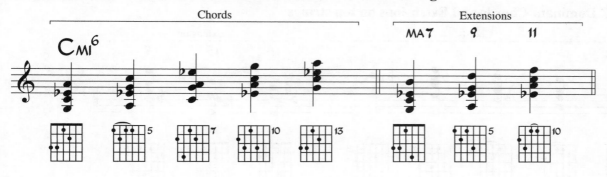

Ex. 4-33 (CD2 - Track #39) shows the tweaked tonic minor chords and extensions on the top set.

Ex. 4-33   Tweaked C Tonic Minor Chords and Extensions on top strings

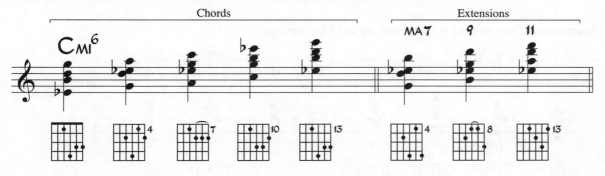

Ex. 4-34 (CD2 - Track #40) shows them on the middle set.

Ex. 4-34   Tweaked C Tonic Minor Chords and Extensions on middle strings

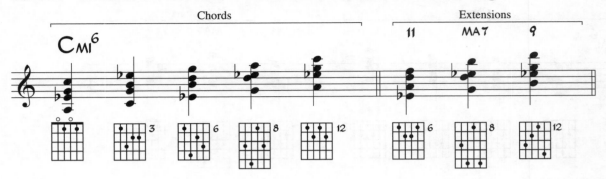

Ex. 4-35 (CD2 - Track #41) shows the C dominant7th chords and extension voicings on the top set of four consecutive strings. The C7 chords are to the left of the double bar, extensions 9, #11, and 13 to the right.

Ex. 4-35   C Dominant Chords and Extensions on top strings

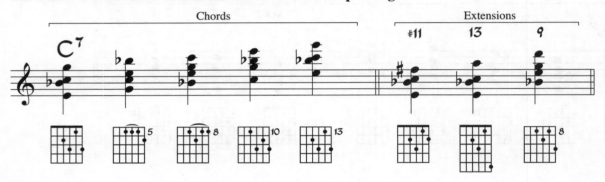

Ex. 4-36 (CD2 - Track #42) shows the same voicings on the middle set.

Ex. 4-36   C Dominant Chords and Extensions on middle strings

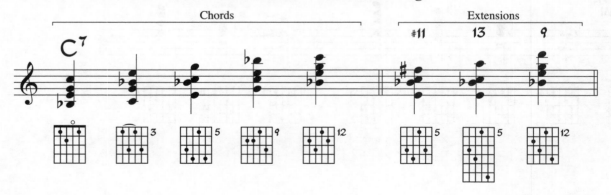

Ex. 4-37 (CD2 - Track #43) shows them on the bottom set.

Ex. 4-37   C Dominant Chords and Extensions on bottom strings

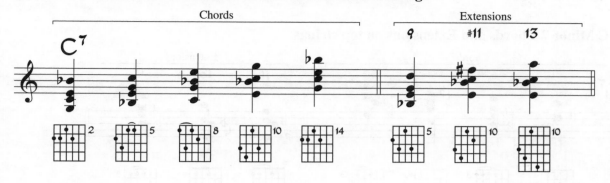

Ex. 4-38 (CD2 - Track #44) shows the tweaked dominant7th chords and extensions on the top set.

Ex. 4-38   Tweaked C Dominant Chords and Extensions on top strings

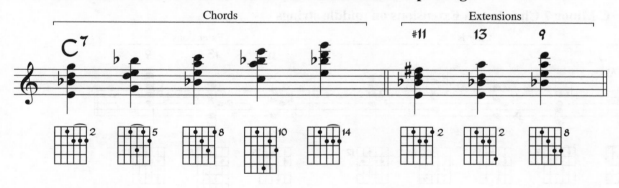

Ex. 4-39 (CD2 - Track #45) shows them on the middle set.

Ex. 4-39   Tweaked C Dominant Chords and Extensions on middle strings

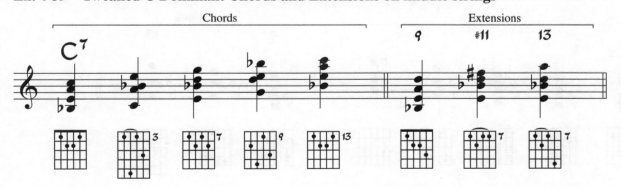

Ex. 4-40 (CD2 - Track #46) shows the C minor7th chords and extension voicings on the top set of four consecutive strings. The Cm7 chords are to the left of the double bar, extensions 9, 11, and 13 to the right.

Ex. 4-40   C Minor 7 Chords and Extensions on top strings

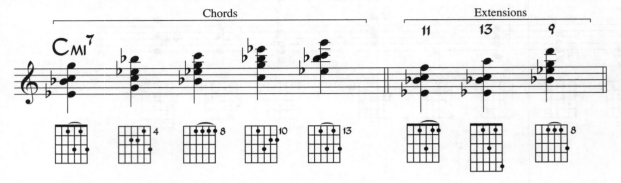

Ex. 4-41 (CD2 - Track #47) shows the same voicings on the middle set.

Ex. 4-41   C Minor 7 Chords and Extensions on middle strings

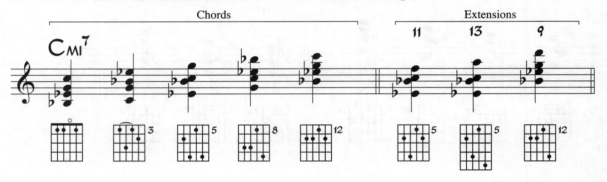

Ex. 4-42 (CD2 - Track #48) shows them on the bottom set.

Ex. 4-42   C Minor 7 Chords and Extensions on bottom strings

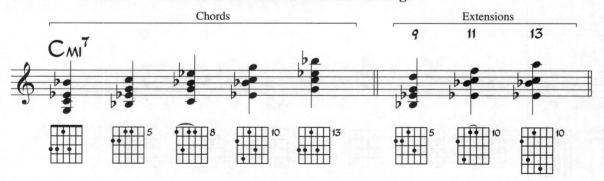

Ex. 4-43 (CD2 - Track #49) shows the tweaked minor7th chords and extensions on the top set.

Ex. 4-43   Tweaked C Minor 7 Chords and Extensions on top strings

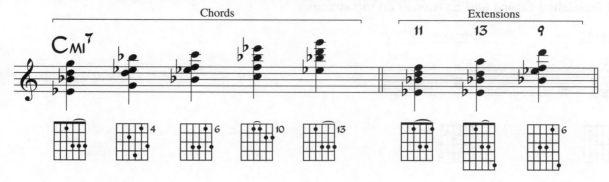

Ex. 4-44 (CD2 - Track #50) shows them on the middle set, with one exception. The first tweaked Cm7 chord can only be played on the bottom set (or you could replace it with the "un-tweaked" version).

Ex. 4-44   Tweaked C Minor 7 Chords and Extensions on middle strings

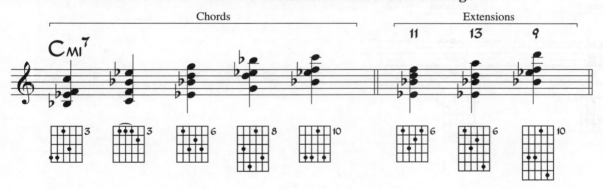

Feel free to mix standard and tweaked voicings as you see fit, but remember to play them up and down and transpose them through all keys.

Now let's take a look at diminished chords. Of course, as you know, they are frequently used to harmonize passing notes in other chords, but they are also frequently used as actual harmonies in themselves, so we should study them as such and also create extension voicings since many notes in actual melodies are diminished chord extensions. Rather than writing them all out like we had to for the other chord types, we'll show one form for each string set since the diminished chord is symmetrical and repeats every three frets (minor 3rds).

Ex. 4-45 (CD2 - Track #51) shows the diminished standard drop 2 voicing and extension voicing for the top set of four consecutive strings.

Ex. 4-45   Diminished Chord and Extension on top strings

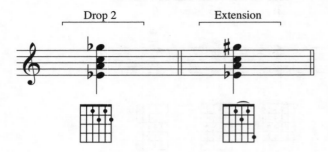

Ex. 4-46 (CD2 - Track #52) shows the same voicings on the middle set.

Ex. 4-46   Diminished Chord and Extension on middle strings

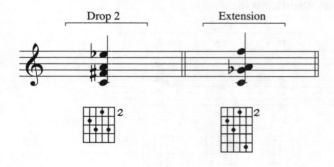

Ex. 4-47 (CD2 - Track #53) shows them on the bottom set.

Ex. 4-47   Diminished Chord and Extension on bottom strings

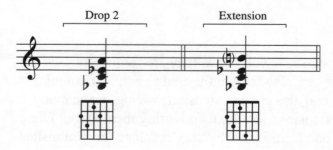

Ex. 4-48 (CD2 - Track #54) shows the diminished tweaked drop 2 and extension voicings on the top set.

Ex. 4-48   Tweaked Diminished Chords and Extensions on top strings

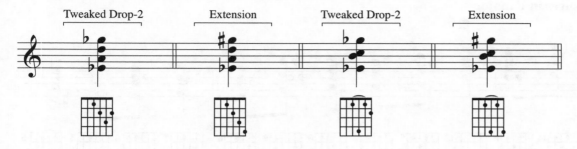

Ex. 4-49 (CD2 - Track #55) shows the practical ones on the middle set.

Ex. 4-49   Tweaked Diminished Chords and Extension on middle strings

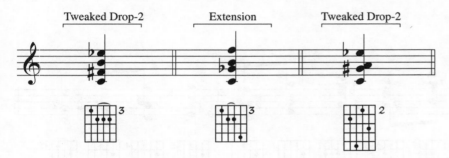

Remember to play all the diminished voicings up and down the fingerboard in minor 3rds and in all keys (which you'll soon discover, if you haven't already, turns out to be only three keys!).

Enclosures and Chromatic Approach Chords

Ex. 4-50 (CD2 - Track #56) shows the enclosures of the major triad tones in the key of C (it's the same as Ex. 3-3).

Ex. 4-50   Enclosures in C major

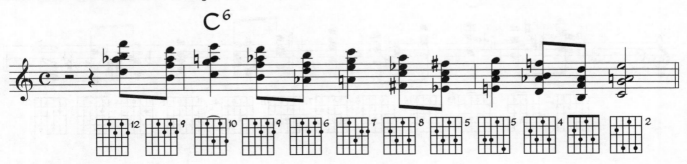

Notice that two chord tones are located on the 1st string and two on the 2nd. Follow this model when transposing to other keys. Ex. 4-51 (CD2 - Track #57) shows the enclosures of the triad tones in the key of F major using the two chord tones per string principle.

Ex. 4-51   Enclosures in F major

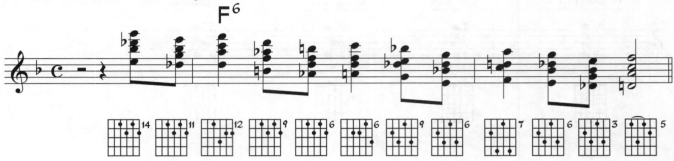

Ex. 4-52 (CD2 - Track #58) shows the enclosures of the triad tones in the key of C minor (it's the same as Ex. 3-5).

Ex. 4-52   Enclosures in C minor

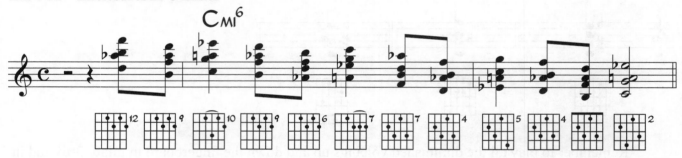

Using the example in F major above (Ex. 4-51) as a model, work out the enclosures for F minor (CD2 - Track #59), then proceed to work them out in every major and minor key.

Ex. 4-53 (CD2 - Track #60) shows enclosures of C major using chromatic approach chords.

Ex. 4-53   Enclosures using Chromatic Approach Chords in C major

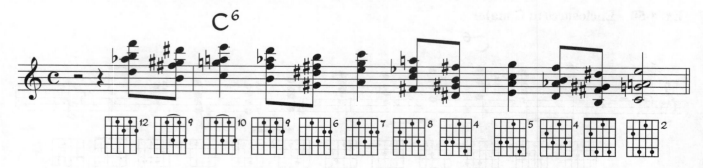

Ex. 4-54 (CD2 - Track #61) shows enclosures of C minor using chromatic approach chords.

Ex. 4-54   Enclosures using Chromatic Approach Chords In C minor

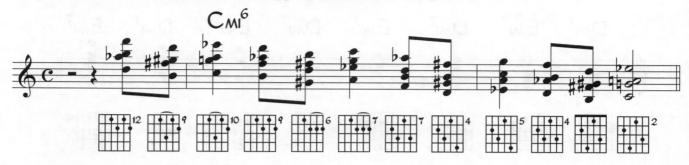

I'm going to leave it up to you to work out the various elaborated enclosures described in Chapter 3. Use all four chord tones of major 6th and minor 6th chords for the elaborated enclosures, but continue to follow the two chord tones per string model and work them out in every key.

Modal Scales

When playing modal scales in drop 2, it's best to start on the "root" of dorian for modes derived from the major scale, and the "root" of locrian #2 for modes derived from the melodic minor scale, because this results in four pairs of identical chord inversions with no duplication of melody notes. Look at Ex. 4-55 (CD2 - Track #62).

Ex. 4-55   A Dorian in Modal Drop-2 on bottom strings

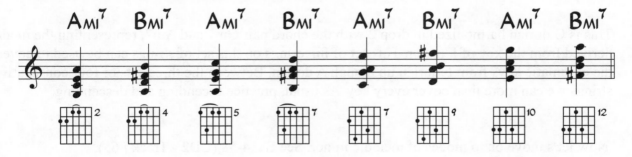

This is A dorian harmonized in drop 2 with the chord pair Am7 and Bm7 (a whole step apart). The Am7 chord has the same notes as C6, and the A dorian mode contains the same notes as the C Lydian mode, and every other mode derived from the key of G major. This set of fingerings on this set of strings can be used to cover chromatic keys from Ab dorian up through Db dorian.

Now look at Ex. 4-56 (CD2 - Track #63).

Ex. 4-56   D Dorian in Modal Drop-2 on middle strings

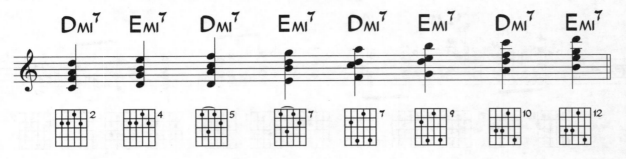

This is D dorian harmonized in drop 2 using the chord pair Dm7 and Em7 (or F6 and G6) representing the modes derived from the key of C major (including F Lydian, G Mixolydian, etc.). This set of fingerings on this set of strings can be used to cover the chromatic keys from Db dorian up through F dorian (at least).

Check out Ex. 4-57 (CD2 - Track #64).

Ex. 4-57   G Dorian in Modal Drop-2 on top strings

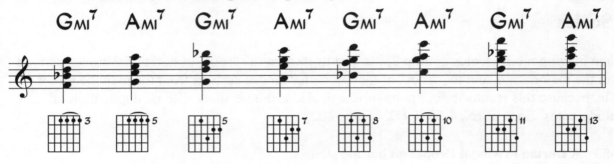

This is G dorian harmonized in drop 2 with the chord pair Gm7 and Am7, representing the modes derived from the key of F major. This set of fingerings on this set of strings can be used to cover the chromatic keys from F dorian up though A dorian. Between the three sets of four consecutive strings we can more than cover every key. As usual, practice ascending and descending.

Now let's move on to modes of melodic minor. See Ex. 4-58 (CD2 - Track #65).

Ex. 4-58   A Locrian #2 in Modal Drop-2 on bottom strings

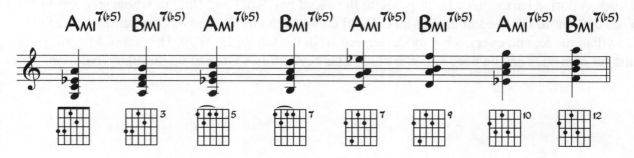

This is A locrian #2 harmonized with the chord pair Am7b5 and Bm7b5 (the same as Cm6 and Dm6), which can be used for all the modes of C melodic minor, including F lydian dominant and B altered dominant, among others (check out Mark Levine's *Jazz Theory Book,* Sher Music Co.). This set of fingerings on this set of strings can be used to cover the chromatic keys from A locrian #2 up through C# locrian #2.

Look at Ex. 4-59 (CD2 - Track #66).

Ex. 4-59   D Locrian #2 in Modal Drop-2 on middle strings

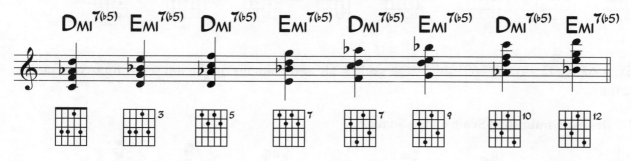

This is D locrian #2 harmonized using the chord pair Dm7b5 and Em7b5 (or Fm6 and Gm6), representing the modes of F melodic minor. This set of fingerings on this set of strings can be used to cover keys chromatically from D locrian #2 up through F locrian #2.

See Ex. 4-60 (CD2 - Track #67).

Ex. 4-60   G Locrian #2 in Modal Drop-2 on top strings

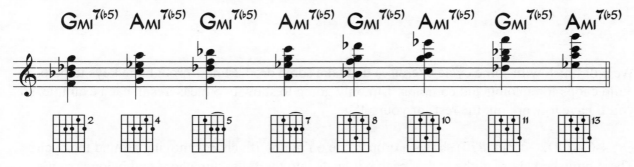

This is G locrian #2 harmonized with the chord pair Gm7b5 and Am7b5 (or Bbm6 and Cm6), representing the modes of Bb melodic minor. This set of fingerings on this set of strings can be used to cover keys chromatically from F# locrian #2 up through A locrian #2. Between the three sets we can cover every key. As always, practice everything both ascending and descending.

Before we move on, let's revisit what I like to call "the Mark Levine drop 2 diminished scale". Look at Ex. 4-61 (CD2 - Track #68, it's Ex. 3-19 from Chapter 3).

Ex. 4-61 Drop-2 Diminished Scale on middle strings

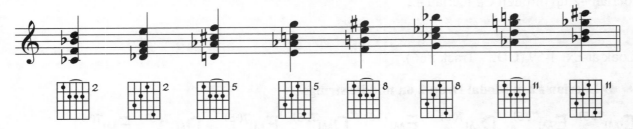

Ex. 4-62 (CD2 - Track #69) shows the same scale and voicings on the top set of four consecutive strings.

Ex. 4-62 Drop-2 Diminished Scale on top strings

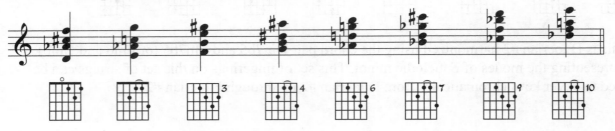

Cycles

We will finish with some cycle exercises that take some drop 2 lines through the keys to help build chops for soloing and comping. I'm only going to show two measures in each example, so you'll have to work out the rest for yourself.

Ex. 4-63 (CD2 - Track #70) shows a drop 2 line on minor 7th chords moving around the cycle. The diminished chord at the end of each bar leads into the following chord and belongs to it's bebop scale.

Ex. 4-63 Drop-2 Minor 7 Cycle

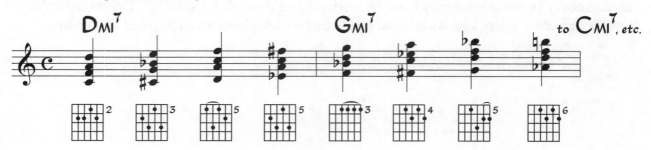

Now work out the rest of the cycle. You can experiment with changing string sets and octaves at various places in the bar. Typically it sounds best to switch octaves on the second or fourth beat of the bar so the diminished chords resolve in the same octave. For example, you might continue 4-63 with a C note on the 1st string followed by D, Eb, and E on the 2nd string. Then continue on Fm7 with F, G, and Ab on the 2nd string, A on the 1st leading to Bbm7 with Bb, C, and Db on the 1st, switching octaves and strings to the 2nd for D leading into Ebm7 (CD2 - Track #71), etc.

Ex. 4-64 (CD2 - Track #72) shows the same thing as example 6-63 but using minor 6th chords.

Ex. 4-64   Drop-2 Minor 6 Cycle

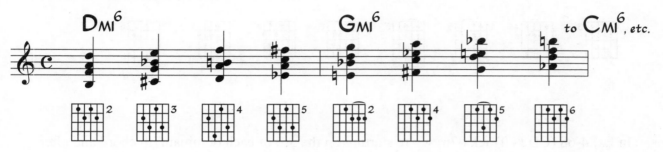

Ex. 4-65 (CD2 - Track #73) shows a drop 2 line on major 6th chords going around the cycle. This example uses two chromatic diminished chords to connect the root and the 3rd of each chord.

Ex. 4-65   Drop-2 Major Cycle from the roots

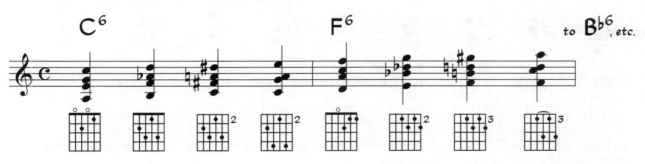

Ex. 4-66 (CD2 - Track #740) shows the same chord progression using inversions of the same two diminished chords, this time connecting the 3rd and the 5th of each chord.

Ex. 4-66   Drop-2 Major Cycle from the 3rds

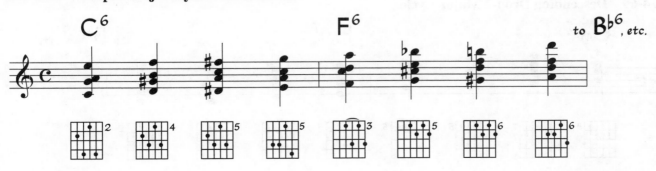

Ex. 4-67 (CD2 - Track #75) shows a drop 2 line on dominant7th chords moving around the cycle using tweaked voicings. Here we use two tweaked diminished voicings connecting the root and 3rd of each dominant7th chord.

Ex. 4-67   Tweaked Drop-2 Dominant Cycle from the roots

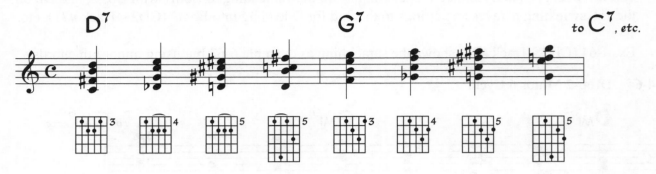

In Ex. 4-68 (CD2 - Track #76) we're starting on the 3rd of each dominant7th chord and after adding the extra diminished chord, we end on a diminished voicing belonging to the following bebop scale, as we did with the minor chords. In this case, however, it could also be analyzed as a dominant7#9 chord (see appendix).

Ex. 4-68   Tweaked Drop-2 Dominant Cycle from the 3rds

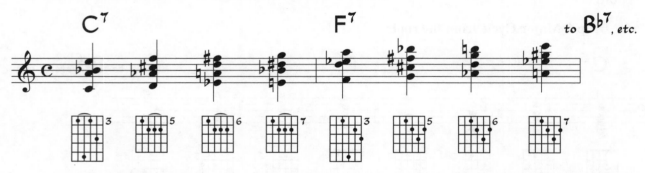

To hear "untweaked" versions (for a more traditional sound) of examples 67 and 68, listen to CD2 - Track #77 and CD2 - Track #78.

Now let's try something new. Play Ex. 4-69 (CD2 - Track #79).

Ex. 4-69   Descending Drop-2 Major Cycle

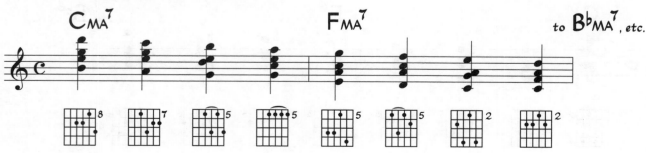

This example features a descending scale line that moves through major7th chords going around the cycle. The line starts on the 2nd step of the scale (the 9th) with the major 7th on the third beat, so these are harmonized with tweaked extension voicings resolving to standard drop 2 chord tone voicings (on the root and 6th). Continue the exercise by going on to Bb major, then Eb etc. Each extension acts as a tension tone resolving to a basic chord tone, so keep each pair of notes (on beats 1 & 2, and on beats 3 & 4) on the same string set in the same octave.

Ex. 4-69 also works on the relative minor7th chords as well. Instead of C major7th, the first chord would be Am7 with the melody starting on the 11th and descending through the 3rd, 9th, and root before moving on to the 11th of Dm7.

Ex. 4-70   Descending Drop-2 Tonic Minor Cycle

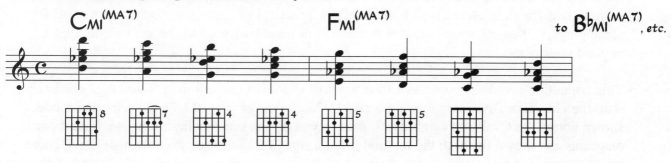

Play Ex. 4-70 (CD2 - Track #80).

This is the same as Ex. 4-69, except using tonic minor-Maj7 chords instead of major chords, so the same instructions apply here. These harmonies belong to the melodic minor scales, so they have varied applications. For instance, this could be Am7b5 going to Dm7b5, or F13#11 going to Bb13#11, or B7alt going to E7alt, etc.

Now we have enough material to keep us practicing for many years to come, but the results should be very rewarding (even after a few weeks or even days). Instead of the usual collection of isolated basic drop 2 chords, we now have the tools to use the drop 2 concept melodically to greatly enhance our melody playing, soloing and comping. So practice hard and have fun.

APPENDIX

Here is a collection of alternate tweaked chord tone and extension tone chord voicings. Some will enable you to cover specific situations that the main text did not address, such as a 13th melody note on a 7b9 chord, for instance. Most are just alternate choices you might try. You can browse through them at your convenience.

Originally the standard voicings were tweaked by keeping the top and bottom notes the same while replacing one or sometimes two notes in the middle. This keeps the bebop scale voice-leading intact. Extension voicings are generally more flexible. The collection here follows the same guidelines in many cases, but often does not. Occasionally some voicings may have extremely difficult stretches which may only be practical in upper positions, or not at all for some players. Please take care not to damage your hand by trying to force a voicing that's beyond your reach.

This collection is only shown as various types of C chords (except the C7 voicings compatible with the C Lydian Dominant mode are also F#7alt voicings from the F# superlocrian mode, shown above the C7 chord symbols). It's up to you do the transposing (although fingerboard diagrams are shown for both the top and middle sets of four consecutive strings). Each chord type is organized by melody notes, first the basic chord tones in order (root, 3rd, etc.), followed by the extension tones.

Alternate Major Chords and Extension Voicings

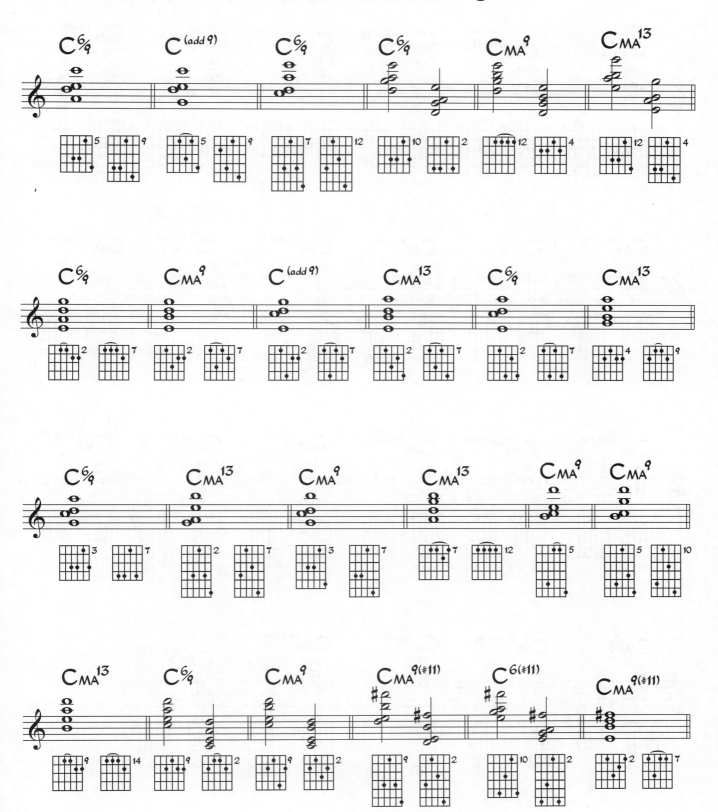

Alternate Tonic Minor Chords and Extension Voicings

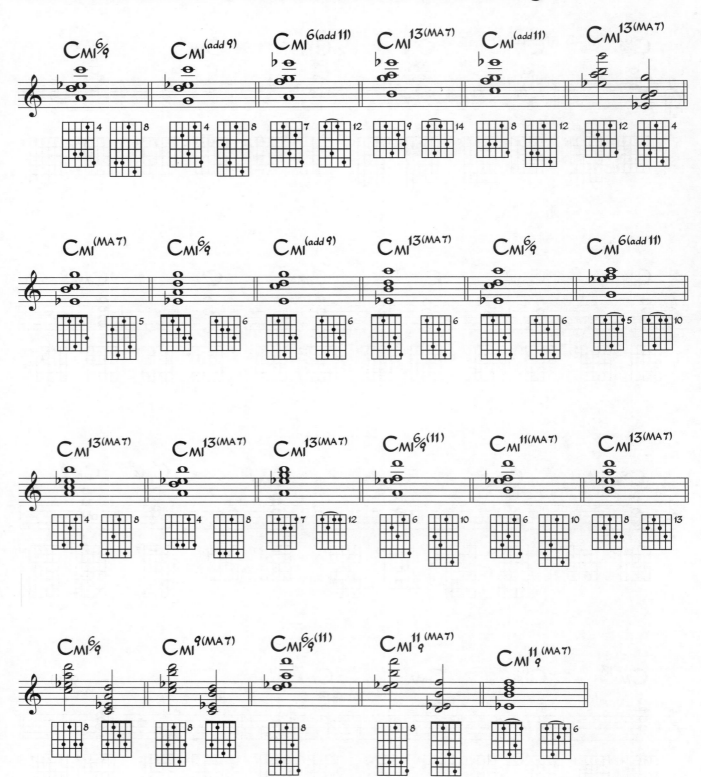

Appendix C - Alternate Minor 7 Chords and Extension Voicings

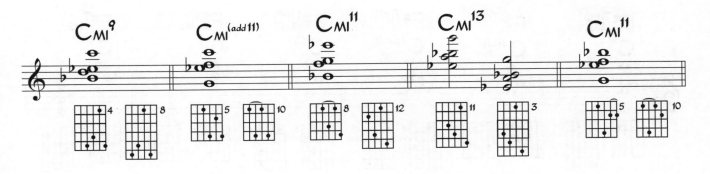

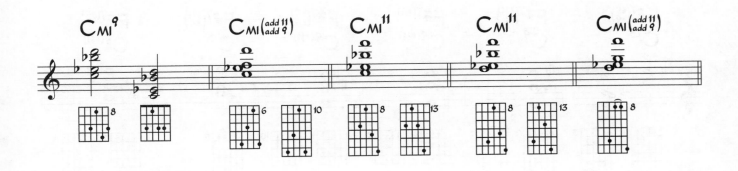

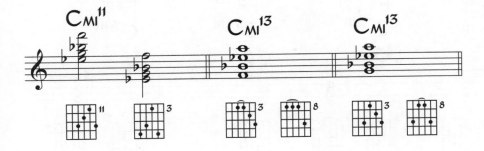

Alternate Dominant Chords and Extension Voicings

Alternate Diminished Scale Dominant Chords and Extension Voicings

SHER MUSIC CO. — The finest in Jazz & Latin Publications

THE NEW REAL BOOK SERIES

The Standards Real Book (C, Bb or Eb)

A Beautiful Friendship
A Time For Love
Ain't No Sunshine
Alice In Wonderland
All Of You
Alone Together
At Last
Baltimore Oriole
Bess, You Is My Woman
Bluesette
But Not For Me
Close Enough For Love
Crazy He Calls Me
Dancing In The Dark

Days Of Wine And Roses
Dreamsville
Easy To Love
Embraceable You
Falling In Love With Love
From This Moment On
Give Me The Simple Life
Have You Met Miss Jones?
Hey There
I Can't Get Started
I Concentrate On You
I Cover The Waterfront
I Love You
I Loves You Porgy

I Only Have Eyes For You
I'm A Fool To Want You
Indian Summer
It Ain't Necessarily So
It Never Entered My Mind
It's You Or No One
Just One Of Those Things
Love For Sale
Lover, Come Back To Me
The Man I Love
Mr. Lucky
My Funny Valentine
My Heart Stood Still
My Man's Gone Now

Old Folks
On A Clear Day
Our Love Is Here To Stay
'Round Midnight
Secret Love
September In The Rain
Serenade In Blue
Shiny Stockings
Since I Fell For You
So In Love
So Nice (Summer Samba)
Some Other Time
Stormy Weather
The Summer Knows

Summer Night
Summertime
Teach Me Tonight
That Sunday, That Summer
The Girl From Ipanema
Then I'll Be Tired Of You
There's No You
Time On My Hands
'Tis Autumn
Where Or When
Who Cares?
With A Song In My Heart
You Go To My Head
And Hundreds More!

The New Real Book - Volume 1 (C, Bb or Eb)

Angel Eyes
Anthropology
Autumn Leaves
Beautiful Love
Bernie's Tune
Blue Bossa
Blue Daniel
But Beautiful
Chain Of Fools
Chelsea Bridge
Compared To What
Darn That Dream
Desafinado
Early Autumn

Eighty One
E.S.P.
Everything Happens To Me
Feel Like Makin' Love
Footprints
Four
Four On Six
Gee Baby Ain't I Good
To You
Gone With The Wind
Here's That Rainy Day
I Love Lucy
I Mean You
I Should Care

I Thought About You
If I Were A Bell
Imagination
The Island
Jersey Bounce
Joshua
Lady Bird
Like Someone In Love
Little Sunflower
Lush Life
Mercy, Mercy, Mercy
The Midnight Sun
Monk's Mood
Moonlight In Vermont

My Shining Hour
Nature Boy
Nefertiti
Nothing Personal
Oleo
Once I Loved
Out Of This World
Pent Up House
Portrait Of Tracy
Put It Where You Want It
Robbin's Nest
Ruby, My Dear
Satin Doll
Search For Peace

Shaker Song
Skylark
A Sleepin' Bee
Solar
Speak No Evil
St. Thomas
Street Life
Tenderly
These Foolish Things
This Masquerade
Three Views Of A Secret
Waltz For Debby
Willow Weep For Me
And Many More!

The New Real Book Play-Along CDs (For Volume 1)

CD #1 - Jazz Classics - Lady Bird, Bouncin' With Bud, Up Jumped Spring, Monk's Mood, Doors, Very Early, Eighty One, Voyage **& More!**
CD #2 - Choice Standards - Beautiful Love, Darn That Dream, Moonlight In Vermont, Trieste, My Shining Hour, I Should Care **& More!**
CD #3 - Pop-Fusion - Morning Dance, Nothing Personal, La Samba, Hideaway, This Masquerade, Three Views Of A Secret, Rio **& More!**
World-Class Rhythm Sections, featuring Mark Levine, Larry Dunlap, Sky Evergreen, Bob Magnusson, Keith Jones, Vince Lateano & Tom Hayashi

The New Real Book - Volume 2 (C, Bb or Eb)

Afro-Centric
After You've Gone
Along Came Betty
Bessie's Blues
Black Coffee
Blues For Alice
Body And Soul
Bolivia
The Boy Next Door
Bye Bye Blackbird
Cherokee
A Child Is Born
Cold Duck Time
Day By Day

Django
Equinox
Exactly Like You
Falling Grace
Five Hundred Miles High
Freedom Jazz Dance
Giant Steps
Harlem Nocturne
Hi-Fly
Honeysuckle Rose
I Hadn't Anyone 'Til You
I'll Be Around
I'll Get By
Ill Wind

I'm Glad There Is You
Impressions
In Your Own Sweet Way
It's The Talk Of The Town
Jordu
Killer Joe
Lullaby Of The Leaves
Manha De Carneval
The Masquerade Is Over
Memories Of You
Moment's Notice
Mood Indigo
My Ship
Naima

Nica's Dream
Once In A While
Perdido
Rosetta
Sea Journey
Senor Blues
September Song
Seven Steps To Heaven
Silver's Serenade
So Many Stars
Some Other Blues
Song For My Father
Sophisticated Lady
Spain

Stablemates
Stardust
Sweet And Lovely
That's All
There Is No Greater Love
'Til There Was You
Time Remembered
Turn Out The Stars
Unforgettable
While We're Young
Whisper Not
Will You Still Be Mine?
You're Everything
And Many More!

The New Real Book - Volume 3 (C, Bb, Eb or Bass clef)

Actual Proof
Ain't That Peculiar
Almost Like Being In Love
Another Star
Autumn Serenade
Bird Of Beauty
Black Nile
Blue Moon
Butterfly
Caravan
Ceora
Close Your Eyes
Creepin'
Day Dream

Dolphin Dance
Don't Be That Way
Don't Blame Me
Emily
Everything I Have Is Yours
For All We Know
Freedomland
The Gentle Rain
Get Ready
A Ghost Of A Chance
Heat Wave
How Sweet It Is
I Fall In Love Too Easily
I Got It Bad

I Hear A Rhapsody
If You Could See Me Now
In A Mellow Tone
In A Sentimental Mood
Inner Urge
Invitation
The Jitterbug Waltz
Just Friends
Just You, Just Me
Knock On Wood
The Lamp Is Low
Laura
Let's Stay Together
Lonely Woman

Maiden Voyage
Moon And Sand
Moonglow
My Girl
On Green Dolphin Street
Over The Rainbow
Prelude To A Kiss
Respect
Ruby
The Second Time Around
Serenata
The Shadow Of Your Smile
So Near, So Far
Solitude

Speak Like A Child
Spring Is Here
Stairway To The Stars
Star Eyes
Stars Fell On Alabama
Stompin' At The Savoy
Sweet Lorraine
Taking A Chance On Love
This Is New
Too High
(Used To Be A) Cha Cha
When Lights Are Low
You Must Believe In Spring
And Many More!

The All Jazz Real Book

Over 540 pages of tunes as recorded by:
Miles, Trane, Bill Evans, Cannonball, Scofield, Brecker, Yellowjackets, Bird, Mulgrew Miller, Kenny Werner, MJQ, McCoy Tyner, Kurt Elling, Brad Mehldau, Don Grolnick, Kenny Garrett, Patitucci, Jerry Bergonzi, Stanley Clarke, Tom Harrell, Herbie Hancock, Horace Silver, Stan Getz, Sonny Rollins, and MORE!

Includes a free CD of many of the melodies (featuring Bob Sheppard & Friends.). $44 list price. Available in C, Bb, Eb

The European Real Book

An amazing collection of some of the greatest jazz compositions ever recorded! Available in C, Bb and Eb. $40

- Over 100 of Europe's best jazz writers.
- 100% accurate, composer-approved charts.
- 400 pages of fresh, exciting sounds from virtually every country in Europe.
- Sher Music's superior legibility and signature calligraphy makes reading the music easy.

Listen to FREE MP3 FILES of many of the songs at www.shermusic.com!

See www.shermusic.com for more information, including a complete list of tunes in all our fake books.
To order, call (800) 444-7437 or fax (707) 763-2038

SHER MUSIC JAZZ PUBLICATIONS

The Real Easy Book Vol. 1
TUNES FOR BEGINNING IMPROVISERS

Published by Sher Music Co. in conjunction with the Stanford Jazz Workshop. $22 list price.

The easiest tunes from Horace Silver, Eddie Harris, Freddie Hubbard, Red Garland, Sonny Rollins, Cedar Walton, Wes Montgomery Cannonball Adderly, etc. Get yourself or your beginning jazz combo sounding good right away with the first fake book ever designed for the beginning improviser.
Available in C, Bb, Eb and Bass Clef.

The Real Easy Book Vol. 2
TUNES FOR INTERMEDIATE IMPROVISERS

Published by Sher Music Co. in conjunction with the Stanford Jazz Workshop. Over 240 pages. $29.

The best intermediate-level tunes by: Charlie Parker, John Coltrane, Miles Davis, John Scofield, Sonny Rollins, Horace Silver, Wes Montgomery, Freddie Hubbard, Cal Tjader, Cannonball Adderly, and more!
Both volumes feature instructional material tailored for each tune. Perfect for jazz combos!
Available in C, Bb, Eb and Bass Clef.

The Real Easy Book Vol. 3
A SHORT HISTORY OF JAZZ

Published by Sher Music Co. in conjunction with the Stanford Jazz Workshop. Over 200 pages. $25.

History text and tunes from all eras and styles of jazz. Perfect for classroom use. Available in C, Bb, Eb and Bass Clef versions.

The Best of Sher Music Co. Real Books
100+ TUNES YOU NEED TO KNOW

A collection of the best-known songs from the world leader in jazz fake books – Sher Music Co.!

Includes songs by: Miles Davis, John Coltrane, Bill Evans, Duke Ellington, Antonio Carlos Jobim, Charlie Parker, John Scofield, Michael Brecker, Weather Report, Horace Silver, Freddie Hubbard, Thelonious Monk, Cannonball Adderley, and many more!
$26. Available in C, Bb, Eb and Bass Clef.

The Serious Jazz Book II
THE HARMONIC APPROACH

By Barry Finnerty, Endorsed by: Joe Lovano, Jamey Aebersold, Hubert Laws, Mark Levine, etc.

- A 200 page, exhaustive study of how to master the harmonic content of songs.
- Contains explanations of every possible type of chord that is used in jazz.
- Clear musical examples to help achieve real harmonic control over melodic improvisation.
- For any instrument. $32. Money back gurantee!

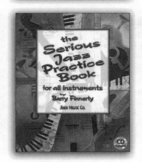

The Serious Jazz Practice Book By Barry Finnerty

A unique and comprehensive plan for mastering the basic building blocks of the jazz language. It takes the most widely-used scales and chords and gives you step-by-step exercises that dissect them into hundreds of cool, useable patterns.
Includes CD - $30 list price.

"The book I've been waiting for!" – Randy Brecker.

"The best book of intervallic studies I've ever seen."
— Mark Levine

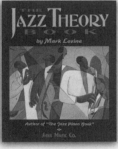

The Jazz Theory Book

By Mark Levine, the most comprehensive Jazz Theory book ever published! $38 list price.

- Over 500 pages of text and over 750 musical examples.
- Written in the language of the working jazz musician, this book is easy to read and user-friendly. At the same time, it is the most comprehensive study of jazz harmony and theory ever published.
- Mark Levine has worked with Bobby Hutcherson, Cal Tjader, Joe Henderson, Woody Shaw, and many other jazz greats.

Jazz Piano Masterclass With Mark Levine
"THE DROP 2 BOOK"

The long-awaited book from the author of "The Jazz Piano Book!" A complete study on how to use "drop 2" chord voicings to create jazz piano magic! 68 pages, plus CD of Mark demonstrating each exercise. $19 list.

"Will make you sound like a real jazz piano player in no time." – Jamey Aebersold

Metaphors For The Musician
By Randy Halberstadt

This practical and enlightening book will help any jazz player or vocalist look at music with "new eyes." Designed for any level of player, on any instrument, "Metaphors For The Musician" provides numerous exercises throughout to help the reader turn these concepts into musical reality.

Guaranteed to help you improve your musicianship. 330 pages – $29 list price. Satisfaction guaranteed!

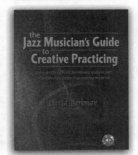

The Jazz Musicians Guide To Creative Practicing
By David Berkman

Finally a book to help musicians use their practice time wisely! Covers tune analysis, breaking hard tunes into easy components, how to swing better, tricks to playing fast bebop lines, and much more! 150+pages, plus CD. $29 list.

"Fun to read and bursting with things to do and ponder." – Bob Mintzer

The 'Real Easy' Ear Training Book
By Roberta Radley

For all musicians, regardless of instrument or experience, this is the most comprehensive book on "hearing the changes" ever published!

- Covers both beginning and intermediate ear training exercises.
- Music Teachers: You will find this book invaluable in teaching ear training to your students.

Book includes 168 pages of instructional text and musical examples, plus two CDs! $29 list price.

The Jazz Singer's Guidebook By David Berkman
A COURSE IN JAZZ HARMONY AND SCAT SINGING FOR THE SERIOUS JAZZ VOCALIST

A clear, step-by-step approach for serious singers who want to improve their grasp of jazz harmony and gain a deeper understanding of music fundamentals.

This book will change how you hear music and make you a better singer, as well as give you the tools to develop your singing in directions you may not have thought possible.

$26 – includes audio CD demonstrating many exercises.

LATIN MUSIC BOOKS, CDs, DVD

The Latin Real Book (C, Bb or Eb)

The only professional-level Latin fake book ever published! Over 570 pages. Detailed transcriptions exactly as recorded by:

Ray Barretto	Arsenio Rodriguez	Manny Oquendo	Ivan Lins
Eddie Palmieri	Tito Rodriguez	Puerto Rico All-Stars	Djavan
Fania All-Stars	Orquesta Aragon	Issac Delgaldo	Tom Jobim
Tito Puente	Beny Moré	Ft. Apache Band	Toninho Horta
Ruben Blades	Cal Tjader	Dave Valentin	Joao Bosco
Los Van Van	Andy Narell	Paquito D'Rivera	Milton Nascimento
NG La Banda	Mario Bauza	Clare Fischer	Leila Pinheiro
Irakere	Dizzy Gilllespie	Chick Corea	Gal Costa
Celia Cruz	Mongo Santamaria	Sergio Mendes	**And Many More!**

The Latin Real Book Sampler CD

12 of the greatest Latin Real Book tunes as played by the original artists: Tito Puente, Ray Barretto, Andy Narell, Puerto Rico Allstars, Bacacoto, etc. $16 list price. Available in U.S.A. only.

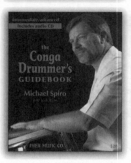

The Conga Drummer's Guidebook By Michael Spiro

Includes CD - $28 list price. The only method book specifically designed for the intermediate to advanced conga drummer. It goes behind the superficial licks and explains how to approach any Afro-Latin rhythm with the right feel, so you can create a groove like the pros!.

"This book is awesome. Michael is completely knowledgable about his subject." – Dave Garibaldi

"A breakthrough book for all students of the conga drum." – Karl Perazzo

Introduction to the Conga Drum - DVD

By Michael Spiro

For beginners, or anyone needing a solid foundation in conga drum technique.

Jorge Alabe – "Mike Spiro is a great conga teacher. People can learn real conga technique from this DVD."

John Santos – "A great musician/teacher who's earned his stripes"

1 hour, 55 minutes running time. $25.

Muy Caliente!

Afro-Cuban Play-Along CD and Book
Rebeca Mauleón - Keyboard
Oscar Stagnaro - Bass
Orestes Vilató - Timbales
Carlos Caro - Bongos
Edgardo Cambon - Congas
Over 70 min. of smokin' Latin grooves!
Stereo separation so you can eliminate the bass or piano. Play-along with a rhythm section featuring some of the top Afro-Cuban musicians in the world! $18.

The True Cuban Bass

By Carlos Del Puerto, (bassist with Irakere) and Silvio Vergara, $22.

For acoustic or electric bass; English and Spanish text; Includes CDs of either historic Cuban recordings or Carlos playing each exercise; Many transcriptions of complete bass parts for tunes in different Cuban styles – the roots of Salsa.

101 Montunos

By Rebeca Mauleón

The only comprehensive study of Latin piano playing ever published.

- Bi-lingual text (English/Spanish)
- 2 CDs of the author demonstrating each montuno
- Covers over 100 years of Afro-Cuban styles, including the danzón, guaracha, mambo, merengue and songo—from Peruchin to Eddie Palmieri. $28

The Salsa Guide Book

By Rebeca Mauleón

The only complete method book on salsa ever published! 260 pages. $25.

Carlos Santana – "A true treasure of knowledge and information about Afro-Cuban music."
Mark Levine, author of The Jazz Piano Book. – "This is <u>the</u> book on salsa."
Sonny Bravo, pianist with Tito Puente – "This will be the salsa 'bible' for years to come."
Oscar Hernández, pianist with Rubén Blades – "An excellent and much needed resource."

The Brazilian Guitar Book

By Nelson Faria, one of Brazil's best new guitarists.

- Over 140 pages of comping patterns, transcriptions and chord melodies for samba, bossa, baiaõ, etc.
- Complete chord voicings written out for each example.
- Comes with a CD of Nelson playing each example.
- The most complete Brazilian guitar method ever published! $28.

Joe Diorio – "Nelson Faria's book is a welcome addition to the guitar literature. I'm sure those who work with this volume wiill benefit greatly"

Inside The Brazilian Rhythm Section

By Nelson Faria and Cliff Korman

This is the first book/CD package ever published that provides an opportunity for bassists, guitarists, pianists and drummers to interact and play-along with a master Brazilian rhythm section. Perfect for practicing both accompanying and soloing.

$28 list price for book and 2 CDs - including the charts for the CD tracks and sample parts for each instrument, transcribed from the recording.

The Latin Bass Book
A PRACTICAL GUIDE
By Oscar Stagnaro

The only comprehensive book ever published on how to play bass in authentic Afro-Cuban, Brazilian, Caribbean, Latin Jazz & South American styles. $34.

Over 250 pages of transcriptions of Oscar Stagnaro playing each exercise. Learn from the best!

Includes: 3 Play-Along CDs to accompany each exercise, featuring world-class rhythm sections.

Afro-Caribbean Grooves for Drumset

By Jean-Philippe Fanfant, drummer with Andy narell's band, Sakesho.

Covers grooves from 10 Caribbean nations, arranged for drumset.

Endorsed by Peter Erskine, Horacio Hernandez, etc.

CD includes both audio and video files. $25.